HAYNES GREAT LOCOMOTIVES SERIES

GREAT WESTERN KINGS

HAYNES GREAT LOCOMOTIVES SERIES

GREAT WESTERN KINGS

KEVIN MCCORMACK

© Kevin McCormack 2011

Kevin McCormack has asserted his right to be identified as
the author of this work.

First published in October 2011 by Haynes Publishing

A catalogue record for this book is available from the
British Library

ISBN 978 0 85733 018 5

Library of Congress catalog card number 2011927864

Published by Haynes Publishing, Sparkford,
Yeovil, Somerset BA22 7JJ, England
Tel: 01963 442030 Fax: 01963 440001
Int. tel: +44 1963 442030 Int. fax: +44 1963 440001
E-mail: sales@haynes.co.uk
Web site: www.haynes.co.uk

Haynes North America Inc.
861 Lawrence Drive, Newbury Park, California 91320, USA

Design and layout by Richard Parsons

Printed and bound in the USA by Odcombe Press LP,
1299 Bridgestone Parkway, La Vergne, TN 37086

Contents

Foreword
by Dennis Howells MBE
Project Manager, Great Western Society No. 6023 restoration team

My first encounter with the 'King' class was as a loco spotter on Platform 1 at Paddington station in the early 1950s, *Ian Allan ABC* book in hand.

From then on, these engines held top place in my admiration of British Railways (BR) locomotives. After school, many hours were spent with my young brother spotting at South Ruislip station on the London–Birmingham line, which was not far from my home. Once I had left school, I became a Signal & Telecommunications (S&T) engineer, leading to a railway career so far spanning 55 years, albeit now part-time!

You can imagine my joy at seeing No. 6000 *King George V* appear on the list of locomotives to be preserved by the British Transport Commission. This was quite a comprehensive list, but one which was to be pruned in due course, with No. 6000 luckily surviving. Quite quickly, the 'King' class disappeared, although No. 6018 *King Henry VI* seemed to be leading a charmed life and we all thought *someone* would buy the engine, but sadly this was not to be.

Five years later, in 1968, I answered the call to join many enthusiasts to help pull out No. 6000 from the Stock Shed at Swindon to enable Bulmers to take charge and overhaul the engine for their use. I made many visits to see the locomotive at Hereford.

My next encounter with No. 6000 was on its return to the main line in 1971.

By then, I was a very young S&T inspector whose area covered Kensington Olympia, where the 'King' was due to be briefly stabled. The London Midland Region, responsible at that time for the route through Olympia, was not too keen on the idea, but a few of us managed to assure the powers that be that the signalling equipment would not be damaged by hot cinders dropping from the ashpan. I was on site every time it steamed and moved, which was Utopia for me, particularly

since I was being paid for my attendance!

I was next involved with 'Kings' when I answered an advertisement placed by the group proposing to save No. 6024 *King Edward I* from Barry scrapyard in 1973. From then on, many hours were spent with the embryo team preparing No. 6024 for the move and collecting spares for it from No. 6023 *King Edward II* (more on this later), which was also lying at Barry. No. 6024 duly arrived at Quainton Road and work began. We were very short of funds in those

Below: In steam days, Paddington station was always a magnet for young trainspotters, as depicted here, on 18 August 1962 when No. 6021 King Richard II was the focus of attention. (Geoff Rixon)

days so progress was slow (sufficiently slow that I was able to buy and restore my own locomotive, pannier tank No. 9466!), and what progress was made was largely funded from our own pockets. As time advanced, I had the honour of testing No. 6024 for the group and, would you believe, the regulator was still stiff (an observation originally made by Kenneth Leech when he drove the locomotive in September 1959 and recorded in his book, *Portraits of 'Kings'*). I became No. 6024's support crew manager on the engine's first outings on the main line, all of this before it was fitted with air brakes, etc.

Suddenly, out of the blue, I was approached by Richard Croucher of the Great Western Society, following a working party I attended at the former Fish Dock at Bristol Temple Meads station, who asked me to assist in loading the remains of No. 6023 for transportation to Didcot, and to lead the restoration for the society.

The first challenge was to prove to the sceptics among the enthusiast fraternity that we were serious in restoring this locomotive to working order, so we decided that an early priority should be the replacement of the wheel set which had been wrecked by a cutter's torch at Barry.

Left: Magnificent but ill-fated No. 6018 King Henry VI stands over the ash pit at Swindon shed on 28 April 1963 when the farewell special took a break there on its Birmingham round trip. (John Beckett)

Left: South Ruislip was a London Underground station, but beyond West Ruislip the WR main line left the Tube trains behind and Ruislip water troughs beckoned. On 5 August 1962, No. 6005 King George II takes refreshment while working the 6.10pm Paddington–Shrewsbury express. (John Cramp)

Above: Hopefully, No. 6000 King George V has not dropped hot coals or ashes at Kensington Olympia station on 5 October 1971 during the famous Bulmers Cider train tour. (Great Western Trust collection)

This turned out to be a nightmare in terms of cost and making it happen, bearing in mind that the final product had to satisfy the railway authorities in order for the locomotive to run on the national network. This was the first main line driving wheel set to be manufactured since BR ceased making their own, and it proved extremely difficult to find a firm prepared to take on the job.

The most thrilling part of the remit was to restore No. 6023 as a single-chimney 'King'. In my opinion, the engines were most elegant in this form, although whether today's quality of coal will remain on the grate has yet to be tested, and we may need two firemen! We wait with baited breath.

As I mentioned earlier, there was so much missing from No. 6023 – it literally consisted only of frames, boiler and wheels – and I, along with others, had removed many parts at Barry for use on No. 6024. These actions were later to haunt me as I had to manage their replacement! My experience gained on No. 6024 was later to prove invaluable for determining material specifications, contractors to use, etc.

A I write, we are nearly there with completing No. 6023 (launch scheduled for 2 April 2011), and I have been able to put my knowledge of signalling to good use in fitting out the locomotive with AWS, TPWS and OTMR devices, which are a requirement of a modern railway.

The fittings on top of the boiler and the cab roof will be full height, but an alternative set will be available. This is because, when operating on the main line, No. 6023 will have to sport a lower cab and chimney, which I have engineered. It will take no more than a few days' work to carry out the substitution. My biggest thrill, however, will be to see the engine steam at its full height with a single chimney – such a beauty!

I feel very proud to have been involved, along with others, in saving and restoring not one but two 'Kings' for the nation.

Dennis Brynley Howells,
MBE, MIRSE, FPWI

Above: Blue is the colour still for No. 6024 King Edward I at Newton Abbot back in 1952, the clue being the white lining. (Michael Bentley collection)

Left: Long fire irons are at the ready for reaching the front of the firebox as No. 6023 King Edward II rests at Old Oak Common around 1937. (J.T. Rutherford/Transport Treasury)

Introduction

The Great Western Railway (GWR) 'King' class 4-6-0s represented the pinnacle of steam power on the GWR and its successor, the Western Region of British Railways (BR), from inception in 1927 through to 1962. In that final year, the entire class of 30 engines was withdrawn as a result of their top-link duties being taken over by diesels, and there being no suitable alternative work for them. Therefore, the 'Kings' did not suffer a lingering death by being downgraded to menial duties (except very occasionally), as did many other classes of express passenger engines. Apart from running-in turns on local passenger or parcels trains following overhaul at Swindon, and some usage on milk trains, they were almost entirely confined to hauling the heaviest express trains on the routes over which they were permitted to run, as well as prestigious special trains, fulfilling these roles with distinction.

On the basis of nominal tractive effort, the 'Kings' were the most powerful and the heaviest 4-6-0 locomotives in Britain. Indeed, many of the other railway companies' larger 4-6-2 Pacifics did not have a greater tractive effort than the 'Kings'. Not for nothing

Right: Coffee bars, juke boxes and girlfriends (not to mention GCE O-levels!) held nothing like the appeal of 'King' locomotives for the author when he photographed (with his primitive camera), No. 6005 King George II crossing over tracks at Princes Risborough in June 1962, during Sunday engineering works. (Author)

Left: No. 6000 King George V stands over the ash pits at Old Oak Common shed sometime between1929, when this locomotive received its smokebox door step iron, and 1933, when its upper lamp bracket was transferred to the smokebox door. (J. Cunningham/ Transport Treasury)

Below: Young railfans congregate at Swindon Stock Shed on 9 August 1968, waiting for ropes to be attached to the front of No. 6000 King George V so that the locomotive can be manually hauled from its isolated resting place. (Author)

did the GWR engines earn the sobriquet the 'Mighty Kings'.

The doyen of the class, No. 6000 *King George V*, visited America in 1927, and was presented with cabside medals and a large bell mounted above the front bufferbeam. As a result, No. 6000 became the GWR's flagship locomotive and often appeared in the company's publicity material.

The GWR's successor, BR's Western Region, also recognised the locomotive's importance, ensuring that, on its withdrawal, it was preserved for posterity and did not suffer the fate of the remainder of the class by being dispatched to a scrapyard (albeit two other members of the class were subsequently rescued and are now restored to running order).

In its afterlife, No. 6000 has another claim to fame. BR introduced a steam ban on its network following the withdrawal of the last standard gauge steam locomotives in August 1968. Earlier in that month, H. P. Bulmer (Cider Makers) Hereford Ltd,

having taken out a sub-lease on the engine which was at that time stored in the Stock Shed at Swindon, arranged for it to be extracted and sent for overhaul.

While the representations of railway enthusiasts for a return to steam running fell on deaf ears, Bulmers succeeded in persuading the BR Board to allow No. 6000 to haul an exhibition train over parts of the former GWR network in October 1971, thereby breaching the steam ban. This opened the door for the return of steam in 1972 to haul special trains (mainly railtours for enthusiasts) and the rest, as they say, is history. This all goes to prove that *King George V* has one of the most fascinating life stories of any British locomotive.

As a lifelong railway enthusiast with a bias towards all things Great Western (largely due to being brought up in Ealing, West London), I am delighted to have been invited by Haynes Publishing to produce this book on the 'Kings', one of my favourite classes of locomotives. I am old enough to remember them in regular service and

Right: The author idled away many happy hours trainspotting from 'Jacob's Ladder', the footbridge at West Ealing under which this up train from Swansea is passing on 16 March 1962, hauled by No. 6012 King Edward VI. (Great Western Trust collection)

'spotted' each one – not too difficult living where I did, with most of the trains they hauled ending up at Paddington.

I witnessed the farewell 'King' special in April 1963, dragging my long-suffering parents to Castle Bar Park Halt on the Greenford Loop to share my misery, and I also helped to provide the manpower to remove No. 6000 from the Swindon Stock Shed in August 1968.

Soon after the demise of the 'Kings', I joined the fledgling Great Western Society, serving as its secretary in the late 1960s/early 1970s. I relinquished the position to devote time to the preservation of a Victorian family saloon carriage (formerly a Thameside bungalow), which is kept at the society's depot at Didcot, home also to a large fleet of GWR locomotives including one of the three surviving 'Kings'. In addition, I am the author of several books on transport subjects, this being my 30th (and first for Haynes).

There have already been many titles devoted to the 'King' class, starting with the Great Western Railway itself in 1928, which described its publication entitled *The 'King' of Railway Locomotives* as being the Book of Britain's 'Mightiest Passenger Locomotive for boys of all ages'. *Haynes Great Locomotive Series: Great Western 'Kings'* contains colour and monochrome images featuring every member of the class during their working lives, most of which have never appeared in print before. The book describes the history of the 'Kings' in depth as well as revealing new information on the class. It also contains footplate experiences and reviews the saving and restoration of the three surviving members. This volume does not cover detailed technical points, apart from the most significant, since these are described in depth in several other publications. The emphasis is on viewing these magnificent locomotives at work, primarily during their operational career on the GWR and BR Western Region.

Kevin R McCormack

Right: Apart from No. 6018's Farewell special which ventured on to the Greenford Loop, 'Kings' would not normally pass through Castle Bar Park Halt, a place much visited by the author in his childhood for the purpose of playing 'Cowboys and Indians' in the adjacent fields and woods! However, on 2 March 1958, services on the West of England main line between West Ealing and Old Oak Common were diverted on to the Birmingham Line via the Loop due to a bridge removal at Acton; one such train being headed by No. 6002 King William IV. (Colin Hogg)

CASTLE BAR PARK HALT

1902–1926
GWR express passenger locomotive design

Express passenger steam locomotive development on the GWR, culminating in the introduction of the 'King' class in 1927, was highly innovative from the turn of the 20th century. By that time, the GWR had escaped from the shadow of its broad gauge origins and was looking to develop faster and more powerful machines in competition with the other main railway companies, particularly those which, by providing alternative routes to the West Country and West Midlands, threatened its business.

The 'Kings'' ancestors

In 1897, George Jackson Churchward was appointed chief assistant to William Dean, the locomotive superintendent (before this post was renamed chief mechanical engineer), and was gradually able to influence Dean away from his more traditional approach, before succeeding Dean in 1902 upon the latter's retirement. At the very end of Dean's tenure, a radical new design of locomotive emerged, No. 100, referred to later.

The standard express passenger locomotives at this time were inside cylindered, outside-framed 4-4-0s and

Churchward realised that this design was beyond further development. With the future emphasis being on heavier trains drawn at higher speeds, it was clear that these needs would best be met by using a larger wheel arrangement which would provide extra adhesion and enable a bigger boiler to be fitted. Consequently, in 1901, Churchward produced drawings for six new standard types of main line locomotive which provided the basis of GWR express passenger locomotive design right up to the end of steam.

The prototype was No. 100, completed

Right: 'Saint' class locomotive No. 2909 Lady of Provence, built in 1906 and an early withdrawal in 1931, hauls a down South Wales express at Kensal Green, near Old Oak Common, around 1920. The train consists of stock in crimson lake livery which became standard on the GWR between 1908 and 1922. (Author's collection)

In February 1902, three months before Dean retired. It was a 4-6-0 with two outside cylinders but, most importantly, its boiler design set the standard for all subsequent GWR locomotive types. The significant feature was the taper which aided efficiency and performance by ensuring that most of the water was concentrated where the greatest heat existed, i.e. at the firebox end, and that the water was sufficiently deep to minimise 'surging' when the locomotive was travelling downhill. No. 100 was later integrated into the 'Saint' class along with Churchward's other two-cylinder prototypes, becoming No. 2900 William Dean. The 'Saints', with their 6ft 8½in driving wheels, were fast machines and the class eventually totalled 77. Built between 1902 and 1913, the last survivor was withdrawn in 1953. None was saved but the Great Western Society is building one at Didcot, utilising some standard components from other locos, which will be capable of running as a 4-6-0 or as a 4-4-2, which some 'Saints' did early in their lives.

Churchward took a particular interest in French and American locomotive developments and did not regard his two-cylinder 4-6-0s as the peak of express locomotive development. He was particularly impressed with the performance of the de Glehn four-cylinder compound Atlantics (4-4-2s) operating in France. He commissioned the construction and purchase of one in 1903 (No. 102 *La France*) for the GWR, to be followed by two slightly larger examples in 1905 (Nos 103 *President* and 104 *Alliance*). Over the years, they were increasingly 'Great Westernised' and gave good service, lasting until the late 1920s, which was a considerable achievement in view of their non-standard characteristics.

Given that the French locomotives were 4-4-2s, Churchward decided to create more realistic comparative trials between his locomotives and the French ones, so he had two of his two-cylinder prototypes, Nos 171 and 172 (later renumbered 2971 and 2972), converted to 4-4-2s, and a dozen built

new as such in 1905. Apart from No. 171 which was reconverted in 1907, they all became 4-6-0s in 1912, by which time Churchward was convinced that this wheel arrangement was preferable, not least because of the greater adhesive weight achieved, which was of particular benefit on the steep gradients in the West Country. He also concluded that

compounding (high-pressure cylinders driving the trailing coupled wheels and low-pressure cylinders driving the leading coupled wheels of the French Atlantics) produced no obvious advantages over his latest designs for simple working, which incorporated improvements in valve gear and steam distribution.

Left: Imported from France, de Glehn compound No. 104 hauls a down express soon after its arrival in Britain and prior to being named Alliance. (Author's collection)

Below: Un-named No. 171, later 'Saint' class No. 2971 Albion, running as a 4-4-2. Built in December 1903 as a 4-6-0, this locomotive became an Atlantic in October 1904 and was reconverted to 4-6-0 wheel arrangement in July 1907. (Author's collection)

Right: When is a 'King' not a 'King'? When it's a 'Star'! No. 4026 King Richard, built in 1909 and withdrawn in 1950, stands at Old Oak Common shed when new. Following the launching of the 6000 'King' class, the locomotive was renamed Japanese Monarch in 1927 and de-named early in the Second World War, for obvious reasons. (Author's collection)

Below: Not named after a mere star or even a planet but it had to be a constellation to befit Britain's most powerful locomotive and the first 4-6-2 Pacific, although this turned out to be a delusion of grandeur. No. 111 The Great Bear takes a rather average-looking train past Old Oak Common soon after its entry into service, in February 1908. (Author's collection)

However, the French locomotives had four cylinders, whereas Churchward's had two cylinders. Consequently, for comparative purposes, he decided to build a four-cylinder machine. So there emerged, in 1906, the prototype, No. 40 *North Star* (later No. 4000), the first member of the 'Star' class, which eventually totalled 73 machines constructed between 1906 and 1923. No.

40 was initially built as a 4-4-2 following the precedent set by the French locomotives, but was converted three years later to 4-6-0 wheel arrangement. This pioneering locomotive can be said to be the grandfather of the 'Kings'. Indeed, by coincidence, ten members of the 'Star' class were named after kings but had their names changed when the separate 'King' class was created.

Churchward envisaged that, with the upsurge of traffic arising from the acceleration of services following the introduction of his new locomotives, express trains would become even heavier and possibly beyond the capabilities of the 'Star' class. In his view, there was a need for engines with larger boilers, and with this in mind, he created, in 1907, an enlarged 'Star', No. 111 *The Great Bear*. This was the first Pacific (4-6-2) in Britain and it became the most powerful locomotive in the country. While it was the GWR's only Pacific, the concept was eventually adopted by other railway companies, although it was almost 15 years before any further main line Pacifics were produced (the Gresley A1s of the Great Northern Railway, and the Raven Pacifics of the North Eastern Railway, the former spawning the class to which the famous locomotive, *Flying Scotsman*, belongs).

Churchward was clearly well ahead of his time but the size and weight of *The Great Bear* restricted its use to the London–Bristol line and its true potential was never realised. Nevertheless, the GWR was proud of this pioneer engine and used it as its flagship in publicity material until the advent of the 'Castle' class in 1923 (see below). By the following year, this unique Pacific was in need of heavy repairs which were not considered justified, at which point it was withdrawn and rebuilt into a 'Castle' class 4-6-0 locomotive, No. 111 *Viscount Churchill*. Churchward's successor, Collett, was criticised by the GWR hierarchy for killing off *The Great Bear*, but, to many others, it seemed a sensible decision based on sound economic considerations: the costs of repairing a one-off locomotive, the performance of which was unexceptional and which had severe route restrictions.

Undaunted by the limitations of *The Great Bear*, both in terms of unspectacular performance (some fireman could not get used to the wide firebox) and route availability, Churchward continued his drive for large-boilered locomotives. In 1919, he proposed fitting larger boilers to the 'Saint' and 'Star' class and to his new mixed-traffic 2-8-0s (the 4700 class),

but the civil engineer vetoed this scheme for the 4-6-0s because of the resultant increase in axle load and consequent restricted route availability, but allowed it for the 4700 class. No. 4700, dating from 1919, which previously carried the standard No. 1 boiler, was fitted with a larger No. 7 boiler in 1921, as were the remaining eight locomotives of this class when they were built in 1921–3. This was Churchward's final achievement before he retired in December 1921, although his wish that the class carry names was not granted. Surviving into the 1960s and used primarily on overnight fast fitted-freights the class was also employed in summer on principal passenger services including, on occasions, titled trains such as the 'Royal Duchy' and 'Torbay Express'.

On Churchward's retirement at the end of 1921, the position of chief mechanical engineer passed to Charles Benjamin Collett who had been Churchward's deputy since 1920. Collett's priority was to produce a locomotive which was more powerful than a 'Star' but had similar route availability, and would therefore be acceptable to the chief engineer. The result was the 'Castle' class, something of a compromise, but a very successful one at that. The boiler was slightly wider than

Left: One of Churchward's new large-boilered mixed traffic 2-8-0s of the 4700 class leaves Paddington in the early 1920s, demonstrating that the use of these powerful locomotives on express passenger trains, despite their relatively small wheels (5ft 8in), was not just a latter day phenomenon. (Author's collection)

that of the 'Star', the firebox was longer and the cylinders larger – modest increases in size which nevertheless revolutionised performance and enabled the 'Castle', the first of which, No. 4073 *Caerphilly Castle*, emerged in August 1923, to snatch from *The Great Bear* the mantle of being Britain's most powerful passenger locomotive. Although purely based on nominal tractive effort, this was no idle claim as the locomotive

exchanges of 1925 demonstrated when the superiority of the 'Castles' against the much larger London & North Eastern Railway (LNER) Pacifics was clearly evident. Testament to the success of the 'Castle' class is the fact that a total of 171 were built over an amazingly long period (from 1923 to 1950), mostly entirely new locomotives, but including some rebuilds from 'Stars' (as well as *The Great Bear*).

Below : Evidence of the GWR's standardisation policy could hardly be clearer in this 1961 view at Cardiff (Canton) shed depicting four passenger locomotive types of varying size. 'Castle' class No. 5061 Earl of Birkenhead almost dwarfs No. 7816 Frilsham Manor and a 'Hall' (possibly No. 5903 Keele Hall) which it is standing between, but the 'King' is the mightiest. (Alan Jarvis)

The need for the 'Kings'

Despite the excellent performance of the new 'Castle' class, there was concern that these locomotives had little in reserve when hauling heavy West of England expresses, particularly if the best coal, which they relied upon, became unavailable, as happened during an industrial dispute in the coal industry in 1926. Furthermore, in that year, the Southern Railway's 'Lord Nelson' class 4-6-0s had seized the mantle of the most powerful passenger engine in Britain from the 'Castle' class. However, the introduction of more powerful locomotives on the GWR was frustrated by civil engineering restrictions, precluding locomotives with an axle loading above 20 tons. This was the reason for the 'Castle' class having to be fitted with a smaller diameter boiler than had been intended, thereby producing an axle loading of 19 tons 14cwt.

Fortuitously, the Government had set up a Bridge Stress Committee in 1919 which reviewed the criteria for setting maximum axle loads in the light of the testing of different types of locomotives over various bridges. The committee concluded that undue emphasis was placed on the dead weight of the locomotive rather than hammer blow forces, the latter being greater (and therefore more harmful) on lighter, two-cylinder locomotives than on heavier four-cylinder locomotives. Consequently, it was possible to relax the restrictions for four-cylinder locomotives, thereby enabling larger locomotive types to be introduced.

The GWR's general manager, Sir Felix Pole, who was becoming increasingly concerned about the company's existing civil engineering restrictions, decided to investigate the matter further and was perplexed to find that in fact all new bridges could accept an axle loading of 22 tons. In addition, there was a small margin of flexibility as regards this limit, and he obtained the chief engineer's agreement to a 22.5 ton limit for four-cylinder locomotives. The chief engineer also committed to ensuring that the few remaining weak bridges on the main line to the West Country would be immediately strengthened. Sir Felix Pole therefore instructed Collett to proceed with the design and construction of a 'Super Castle' class (subsequently becoming the 'King' class).

Collett's remit was to design a locomotive which was considerably more powerful than the 'Castle'.

Furthermore, it had to have a nominal tractive effort much greater than that of the 'Lord Nelson' class in order to provide some leeway in the event of other railway companies inevitably producing more powerful locomotives. Admittedly, high nominal tractive effort alone was not necessarily evidence of a more powerful or efficient engine – this depended on the balance between tractive effort (hauling power) and adhesive weigh. Comparative trials of locomotives, as happened in 1925 between the GWR and the LNER, were probably the only true measure. Nevertheless, nominal tractive effort was the measure of power that railway publicity departments relied upon. The fact that 'Castles' in as-built condition were undoubtedly better performers than the 'Lord Nelsons' in their original state, despite their lower tractive effort, could not be effectively publicised.

There was intense rivalry between the 'Big Four' railway companies formed from the grouping of the myriad of companies that existed before 1923, and they were all very publicity conscious. The GWR was extremely concerned at the emergence of the Southern's 'Lord Nelson' class to claim the title of being Britain's most powerful passenger locomotive. This honour had remained with the GWR, having passed in 1923 from *The Great Bear* (tractive effort

Below: Big brother meets smaller sibling at Paddington. No. 6001 King Edward VII and No. 5021 Whittington Castle wait on the starting blocks with the 12pm and 12.3pm departures on 28 July 1934.
(Transport Treasury collection)

29,430lb) to the 'Castle' (tractive effort 31,625lb). (Although, from 1921, the large-boilered 4700 class engines had a higher tractive effort (30,460lb) than *The Great Bear*, they were not officially passenger engines, being classified as mixed traffic.)

Now the 'Castle' class no longer had the highest tractive effort of all express passenger locomotives. The prestige which the GWR's publicity department had built up over the years, culminating in the relatively diminutive 'Castle'

outperforming the larger and heavier LNER Pacifics in the exchange trials of 1925, would inevitably diminish. Consequently, the GWR was determined to reclaim the title of having Britain's most powerful passenger locomotive as quickly as possible. The tractive effort of the 'Lord Nelsons' was 33,510lb. The new locomotive had to exceed the magic 40,000lb mark to ensure that the GWR did not simply recapture the title but retain it exclusively for the

foreseeable future. In the event, this was for only five years, because the 'Kings' tractive effort was matched by the London Midland & Scottish (LMS) 'Princess Royal' Pacifics designed by William Stanier shortly after he left the GWR (and which some people regard as nothing more than an enlarged 'King'!). In addition, Sir Felix Pole required the first 'King' to be ready to haul heavier trains on the West of England main line at the start of summer 1927.

Above: Spectators study Southern Railway 'Lord Nelson' class No. 861 Lord Anson. This company, which suffered from a poor public image at the time, took every opportunity to promote the 'Nelsons' as Britain's most powerful passenger engines, but they held the tractive effort top spot for barely a year. ('Topical' Press Agency/Author's collection)

Original design and specification

Although Collett was regarded by some engineers as unimaginative, tending to continue current practice rather than experiment, he had little choice when it came to creating the new locomotive type, for which he had been given barely a year to design, build and put into service. Another attempt at producing a Pacific was therefore out of the question and so Collett stuck with the basic Churchward design of 4-6-0. In fact, the engineering drawings for the 'King' class were not received in the works until the end of December 1926, and construction had to be very fast to ensure that there was a completed engine ready by the following summer.

The design of the 'King' class was based on a narrow firebox, a boiler which provided good circulation, relatively high boiler pressure, and a moderate level of superheat, all of which combined to make efficient use of the high calorific value of Welsh coal and reduce mechanical and boiler wear. Collett saw no need to depart from these general principles and simply designed an enlarged 'Castle'. Unfortunately, even with a bigger boiler and increased boiler pressure, together with larger cylinders, the nominal tractive effort of the new class would only reach 39,000lb. However, by reducing the size of the driving wheels from the standard size for express engines of 6ft 8½in to 6ft 6in, the tractive effort was increased to 40,300lb.

Critics of the GWR, and the 'King' class in particular, argue that wheel sizes were reduced purely for publicity purposes, i.e. to revive the boast of having Britain's most powerful passenger locomotive. This may have been a convenient outcome, but would hardly justify the considerable additional costs of producing non-standard wheel sizes. A more reasoned view is that the wheel size was reduced to allow for the fitting of a larger boiler while keeping the locomotive within the loading gauge. Furthermore, smaller wheels would enable higher average speeds to be maintained on steep gradients such as the South Devon banks.

As if Collett were not under enough pressure already from Sir Felix Pole to produce the new type as quickly as possible, a further edict arrived. An American railway enthusiast, acting on behalf of the Baltimore & Ohio Railroad, had attended the Stockton & Darlington Railway Centenary celebrations in 1925 and had met Sir Felix Pole. The visitor had been sent to provide feedback on the event to the B&O Railway which was planning a centenary event of its own in 1927, and the question of a British locomotive attending was raised. Sir Felix Pole had readily agreed to provide a locomotive and at that time had a 'Castle' in mind. However, with an enlarged 'Castle' now on the drawing board, Sir Felix told Collett that a member of the new class must be sent and, furthermore, that the Americans were expecting it to do more than just take part in a parade. It was also to undertake some main line running and, with the new locomotive representing British railway engineering, nothing must go wrong.

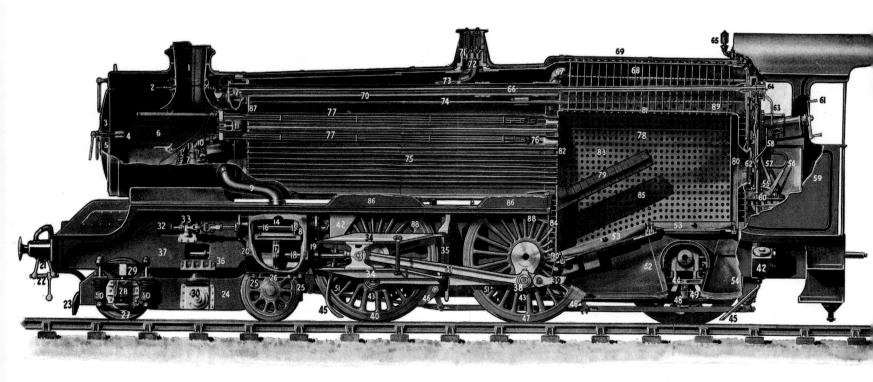

Left: The lower part of the firebox of No. 6023 King Edward II, showing the new ashpan, prior to its being fitted into the frames. The large aperture is to accommodate the rear driving wheel axle. The ashpan was constructed on the basis of measurements taken of No. 6000. (Frank Dumbleton/ Great Western Society)

With the B&O centenary celebrations due to start on 24 September 1927, the locomotive would need to be shipped to the USA during the previous month. It would first need to be tested thoroughly on the GWR main line, which meant that construction needed to be completed by the end of June; also the remaining weak bridges on the London–Plymouth line had to be strengthened or rebuilt by then. True, summer 1927 had been the original timescale, but it left no margin for unforeseen delay. It was all hands to the pumps at Swindon Works to complete a locomotive by the deadline. The construction teams raced against each other and it is believed that the first engine to be completed (No. 6000) was actually the second to be started.

At the same time, consideration was being given to suitable names for this 'Super Castle' class. Thought was given to naming the new engines after cathedrals but, with the impending American visit, something more obviously patriotic was preferred. It was therefore decided to name them after British kings, in descending order, with the first locomotive bearing the name of the current monarch, King George V, who had visited Swindon Works (and driven a 'Castle') in 1924, and who was likely to be agreeable to this proposal. Unlike the 'Stars' which simply stated the different names, e.g. King George, King Henry, etc., the monarchs would now be distinguished by their number as well as their name.

"KING" CLASS FOUR-CYLINDER EXPRESS LOCOMOTIVE
GREAT WESTERN RAILWAY

1 Chimney.	35 Guide Bar Bracket.	70 Internal Steam-pipe.
2 Blower Connection.	36 Bogie Bearing Angle.	71 Safety Valves.
3 Smoke-box Door Baffle.	37 Engine Main Frame.	72 Clack Box.
4 Door-fastening Dart.	38 Crank Pin.	73 Water Delivery Trays.
5 Smoke-box Door.	39 Coupling Rod.	74 Longitudinal Stays.
6 Smoke-box.	40 Leading Driving Wheel.	75 Fire Tubes.
7 Blast Pipe.	41 Connecting Rod.	76 Steam Superheaters.
8 Steam Port.	42 Sand-boxes.	77 Superheater Flue Tubes.
9 Outside Steam-pipe.	43 Driving Wheel Springs.	78 Firebox.
10 Steam-pipe from Superheater.	44 Axle-box Horns.	79 Brick Arch.
11 Superheater Header.	45 Sand-pipes.	80 Firebox Back Plate.
12 Regulator Valve.	46 Brake Shoes.	81 Firebox Crown.
13 Blast Nozzle.	47 Middle Driving Wheel.	82 Firebox Tube Plate.
14 Steam Chest.	48 Vacuum Brake Train Pipe.	83 Firebox Stays.
15 Piston Valve.	49 Trailing Wheel Spring.	84 Firebox Threat Plate.
16 Valve Rod.	50 Covers for Indiarubber Pads.	85 Expansion Bracket Position.
17 Piston.	51 Equalizer Guards.	86 Splashers.
18 Piston Rod.	52 Ash-pan.	87 Smoke-box Tube Plate.
19 Stuffing Gland.	53 Fire Bars.	88 Balance Weight.
20 Front Cylinder Cover.	54 Damper Doors.	89 Fusible Safety Plug.
21 Buffer.	55 Ash-pan Damper Handles.	90 Foundation Ring.
22 Screw Coupling.	56 Cylinder Drain Handle.	91 Tender Wheel Spring.
23 Bogie Guard Iron.	57 Sand Gear Handle.	92 Spring Hanger.
24 Bogie Frame.	58 Fire Door Handle.	93 Brake Block.
25 Cylinder Drain Cocks.	59 Cab Side.	94 Brake Rod.
26 Cylinder.	60 Footplate.	95 Water Scoop.
27 Bogie Wheel.	61 Reversing Gear Handle.	96 Water Inlet Pipe.
28 Outside Bogie Axlebox.	62 Fire Door.	97 Deflector Dome.
29 Bogie Spring.	63 Regulator.	98 Rear Buffer.
30 Bogie Side-Control Spring Housing.	64 Blower Valve.	99 Tender Frame.
	65 Whistle.	100 Front Tender Buffer.
31 Crosshead.	66 Regulator Rod.	101 Brake Handle.
32 Inside Cylinder Steam Chest.	67 Mouth of Steam-pipe.	102 Water Pick-up Handle.
33 Valve Spindle Rocker.	68 Vertical Stays.	103 Axlebox.
34 Guide Bars.	69 Boiler Casing.	104 Vacuum Brake Reservoir.

The high tractive effort of the 'Kings' was, of course, not solely due to the reduction in size of the driving wheels. Compared with the 'Castles', the 'Kings'' firebox was 16 per cent larger, with a consequent increased grate area (the distance from the firehole door to the front of the firebox was a massive 10ft 7in, requiring considerable strength with the shovel). Also, the boiler barrel was lengthened, broadened in diameter and strengthened to withstand a boiler pressure of 250lb. This was 25lb higher than other GWR express locomotives, and it was these factors (enlarged boiler and firebox), combined with bigger cylinders, that were the main contributors to the high tractive effort. The three-cylinder LMS 'Royal Scot' 4-6-0s introduced in the same year as the 'Kings', also had a boiler pressure of 250lb but, with smaller cylinders, could only produce a tractive effort of 33,150lb.

The 'Kings'' four cylinders (two inside and two outside) were of equal dimensions but the increase in size over the 'Castle' design would have created clearance problems if the standard bogie design had been adopted. To overcome the problem, the leading bogie axle was fitted with outside bearings and framing to provide ample room for the inside cylinders and valve chests, which were set well forward. However, the same design could not be used for the trailing bogie axle as this would have fouled the outside cylinders which were set back in order to drive the middle driving wheels, hence the need for the rear bogie wheels to be fitted with inside bearings. The outside frame to the leading pair of bogie wheels provided the 'King' with a distinctive and easily identifiable external feature.

The longer wheelbase necessitated by the increases in size meant that longer connecting rods were fitted. The power produced by these enlargements over the 'Castle' was intended, not to achieve fast running as such, but to enable trains weighing up to 360 tons to be hauled over the South Devon banks between Newton Abbot and Plymouth without need for double-heading. ('Castles' were

LOCOMOTIVE CAB FITTINGS

This photograph indicates the fittings of a modern express engine. The numbers are explained in the following key :

1. Train heating steam valve.	9. Main regulator with drifting valve attachment.	17. Coal watering hose cock.
2. Auxiliary steam valve for exhaust injector.	10. Vacuum brake handle and valve.	18. Damper handles.
3. Steam valve for live injector.	11. Steam ejector handle.	19. Reversing screw and handle.
4. Vacuum brake gauge.	12. Blower valve.	20. Front and back sanders.
5. Boiler steam gauge.	13. Hydrostatic cylinder lubricator.	21. Cylinder drain cock lever.
6. Train heating steam gauge.	14. Firehole door lever.	22. Live steam injector water valve handle.
7. Water gauge (blow-down cock at foot).	15. Axlebox lubricator.	23. Automatic train control apparatus.
8. Water test cocks.	16. Exhaust injector water cock handle.	X. Washout plugs.

limited to 315 tons). The objective was to create economies of working, eliminate delays caused by attaching pilots, and enable higher average speeds of around 60mph to be achieved.

The 'Kings' are 68ft 2in long over the buffers, including the tender, and the total weight of the locomotive in working order, i.e. with water in the boiler but without the tender, is 89 tons. The total weight on the six 6ft 6in diameter driving wheels is 67.5 tons, giving a load of 22.5 tons on each of the three axles, and the 3ft diameter bogies wheels carry the remaining weight of

21.5 tons. The tender is designed to carry 4,000 gallons of water and 6 tons of coal, and weighs 46 tons 14cwt when full, bringing the total weight of the engine and tender combined to 135 tons 14cwt. The wheelbase is 29ft 5in of which 16ft 3in is rigid. There is a unique method of providing independent springing of the bogie wheels as a result of the unusual bogie design referred to above, resulting in the leading bogie wheels having axle boxes and bearings placed outside the bogie frames while the trailing wheels had axle boxes and bearings inside the frames. Unfortunately, this unusual

design was to cause problems when the 'Kings' first entered service and also towards the end of their working lives.

The diameter of the four cylinders was officially 16.25in, with a stroke of 28in, although only Nos 6000–6005 were built with cylinders of this size, the remainder of the class being provided with 16in diameter cylinders. The outside cylinders drive the middle pair of coupled wheels while the inside cylinders drive the leading pair.

The positioning of the inside cylinders ahead of the outside cylinders enables the connecting rods to be of the same

Right and far right: Two views facing forwards and made possible by the absence of the boiler. First, looking down on No. 6023's crank axle and showing the components, including the big ends, which connect the axle of the leading driving wheels to the inside cylinders and valve gear. Secondly, looking up towards the back of the inside cylinders, this time from underneath and ahead of the big ends, showing No. 6023's inside connecting rods on the left and right. (Frank Dumbleton/Great Western Society)

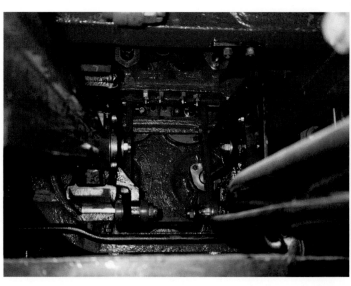

length and helps to simplify the balancing. The divided drive has the advantage over undivided drive of avoiding excessive stress falling on a single axle. The boiler (No. 12 type) has a conical barrel 16ft long and 6ft maximum diameter and the Belpaire-type firebox has an external length of 11ft 6in and a grate area of 34.3sq ft. The heating surface amounts to 2,514sq ft and the boiler pressure is 250lb per sq in (25lb above the Swindon norm). The tractive effort at 85 per cent of the boiler pressure is 40,300lb. The valve gear is fitted between the frames, the outside cylinders being worked by rocker arms, which reduces the number of eccentrics normally used in Walschaerts link motion, but makes lubrication an unpleasant task for the poor soul who has to descend into a pit to reach the oiling points at some unearthly hour of the morning!

Left: The front end of No. 6024 showing the inside cylinder and valve casting, the ends of the valves (in black), and the saddle for supporting the smokebox, which has been removed. (Mike Pope)

Above: The photographer is clearly obsessed with No. 6000's front end at Newbury Racecourse station on 27 October 1962, and wants to get a closer view! At the top on the left is the valve chest and on the right, beneath the lubrication pipes, is the vacuum retaining valve. The dishing on the front frame to accommodate the leading bogie axle can also be seen. (Mike Pope)

Charles Collett

Charles Benjamin Collett was born on 10 September 1871 at Grafton Manor in Worcestershire, the son of a journalist, and was educated in London. After leaving university he worked briefly for a marine engineering firm before joining the GWR in May 1893 as a junior draughtsman in the Swindon drawing office. In 1900, he became Assistant Manager of the Locomotive Works, but had to wait 12 years before being appointed General Manager of the Works. During this time, Collett improved workshop practices, leading to reductions in manufacturing costs, and was therefore well placed to become Deputy to the Chief Mechanical Engineer, G.J. Churchward, in May 1919, and whom he succeeded in January 1922 on the latter's retirement.

He has been criticised in some quarters for not being sufficiently innovative, thereby allowing the other three main line railway companies to overtake the GWR in terms of modern locomotive design, as his tenure progressed. It cannot be denied that Collett's locomotives, which consisted of some 20 different classes, were mostly little more than updated versions of Churchward's designs, and his resistance to higher superheating does seem short-sighted. Nevertheless, his aesthetically handsome locomotives served the GWR and BR Western Region well, lasting through to dieselisation, and he was responsible for two iconic classes, the 'Kings' and the 'Castles'. The former matched the performance of the other companies' larger Pacifics and the latter, influencing LMS and LNER locomotive design.

Collett's responsibilities extended beyond locomotive design to rolling stock and there was certainly some innovation as regards

carriages. For a start, he reduced seven different types of bogies to one standard type. He should also be remembered for his modern carriage designs, which included the famous Centenary stock for the 'Cornish Riviera Express', the Super Saloons for the Plymouth boat train services, and of course, his futuristic diesel railcars (this time with attractive streamlining – see picture of No. 4).

He was a quiet man, lacking the charisma of his predecessor, Churchward, and took little part in Swindon life, whether within the Works or in the town itself. However, for almost his entire career as CME, he had been a widower, his wife having died unexpectedly in 1923 after a short illness, and this tragedy must inevitably have affected his attitude and personality.

Collett retired as CME in 1941, just short of his 70th birthday, being succeeded by F.W. Hawksworth. Unlike his predecessor, Churchward, who, in retirement, continued to live near the railway at Swindon (and was unfortunately killed by one of his successor's engines, No. 4085 *Berkeley Castle*), Collett left the town and moved to Wimbledon. He died, aged 80, on 5 April 1952, but Swindon has not forgotten him. While he was still CME, Swindon Borough Council honoured him by naming a new road, Collett Avenue, in 1938, which just happens to run parallel to Churchward Avenue!

GWR diesel railcar No. 4 seen at Didcot shed in 1969. (Author)

1927–1930
The debut of the 'King' class

The pioneer locomotive from the initial production line of six engines, No. 6000 *King George V*, was completed at Swindon Works in early June 1927 (the other five following very soon after), and it was declared operational with effect from 29 June. Its first public appearance was on 1 July when it was put on display at Paddington station and it then went on tour to several other major stations across the GWR system. The engine, now proclaimed to be the most powerful passenger locomotive in Britain, generated enormous media and public interest.

Entry into service

Following its exhibition, No. 6000 returned to Swindon for the temporary fitting of a Westinghouse brake system which was required for working trains in America. Then, on 20 July, the locomotive made its maiden public journey hauling the 'Cornish Riviera Express' non-stop from Paddington to Plymouth, climbing Dainton and Rattery banks in South Devon unaided. The train, having 'slipped' two coaches at Westbury, weighed 350 tons full, making this the heaviest train at that time to be worked over these banks by a single engine. This inaugural run also produced a fast timing, with 4.5min being clipped from the scheduled time of 247min, despite a 5min delay in West London due to engineering works. The 155.25 miles between Slough and Exeter were covered at an average speed exceeding 61.3mph.

Another impressive performance

Right: No Health and Safety worries here as No. 6000 King George V is invaded by a curious public while on display at Plymouth in early July 1927, before entry into service. ('Topical' Press Agency/Author's collection)

occurred two days later when No. 6001 *King Edward VII* hauled the 'Cornish Riviera Express' but, with an extra coach added, making a full load over the Devon banks of 400 tons, a pilot engine was added, resulting in the train arriving at Plymouth on time rather than ahead of schedule. However, hauling a full load of 480 tons as far as Westbury, the train had been over 1.5min ahead of schedule at this point and 3min better than No. 6000 hauling a lighter load (425 tons full as far as Westbury).

Although these performances on the 'Cornish Riviera Express' were impressive, bearing in mind that the crew were unfamiliar with this type of engine, they were perhaps not as spectacular as some may have hoped. Given the significantly increased tractive effort of the 'Kings' (40,300lb) over the 'Stars' (27,800lb) and the fact that 'Stars' could already slice three minutes off the 'Cornish Riviera Express' schedule, and taking into account the teething problems experienced with the 'Kings'' bogie wheels (see below), some critics wondered if the 'Kings' had been produced purely for publicity purposes. They appeared to be adding little value,

Left and above: Piloting the heaviest trains over the Devon banks remained normal practice throughout the steam era, as illustrated by these two views taken on 2 August 1959 near Dainton Tunnel. Nos 7820 Dinmore Manor and 6029 King Edward VIII head the up 'Cornish Riviera Express' while Nos 5977 Beckford Hall and 6015 King Richard III are about to enter the tunnel with another up express. (John Beckett)

Right: The down 'Cornish Riviera Express' is seen near Bedwyn in August 1929 hauled by No. 6011 King James I. (Dr Ian C. Allen/ Transport Treasury)

A recorded working of the down 'Cornish Riviera Express' in July 1929 by No. 6000 *King George V* illustrates this point. Hauling 14 coaches weighing 510 tons full, as far as Westbury (405 tons beyond), the train was ahead of schedule all the way from passing Reading and arriving at Plymouth three minutes early despite several slacks during the journey. Although the train exceeded the maximum unassisted load, no pilot was taken over the Devon banks.

Another excellent running of the down 'Cornish Riviera Express' was recorded on 1 September 1930 with No. 6013 *King Henry VIII* in charge. The train, comprising 16 coaches weighing 580 tons full as far as Westbury (then reduced to 475 tons full), was two minutes behind schedule on passing Reading, despite exceeding 70mph twice before that point. However, subsequent hills were climbed with relative ease considering the extremely heavy load, with 83.5mph attained near Lavington, and Taunton was passed one minute early despite four slacks.

There is no question that the 'Kings'' high tractive effort enabled them to accelerate away from a standing start with heavy loads and take these with ease up steep gradients, the only limitation being the endurance of the fireman.

Below: Following the fitting of its smokebox step iron in 1929, No. 6000 King George V brings a down express into Plymouth North Road on washing day. (Dr Ian C. Allen/ Transport Treasury)

particularly since better quality coal was now available, thereby improving the performance of the 'Castles' and 'Stars'. Nevertheless, it cannot be denied that the introduction of the 'Kings' enabled heavier trains to be taken over the West of England main line. For standard timekeeping,

'Kings' were allowed 500 tons between Paddington and Taunton and 360 tons between Taunton and Plymouth (unaided) compared with 455 tons and 315 tons respectively for a 'Castle', 420 tons and 288 tons for a 'Star', and 392 tons and 252 tons for a 'Saint'.

However, returning to 1927, despite these initial promising performances, there were reports that the 'Kings' were apt to roll at high speed and this problem manifested itself in a dramatic fashion on 10 August at the same time as No. 6000 was rolling on the high seas heading for North America. On that date the bogie wheels of No. 6003 *King George IV*, which was hauling the down 'Cornish Riviera Express', became derailed near Midgham in Berkshire while travelling at about 60mph.

Fortunately, the accident happened on straight track and the driver was able to stop the train safely. Had it happened over points the train could have overturned, with disastrous consequences. Clearly, some urgent modifications to the springing were necessary, not least because of No. 6000's intended main line running in America, where the same problem experienced by No. 6003 at Midgham might occur.

Following the Midgham derailment, tests were immediately carried out on the

Below left: Two of the early locomotives fitted with the interim springing arrangement following the Midgham incident were Nos 6001 King Edward VII and 6004 King George III. No. 6001 is seen at Paignton on the 7.36am Monday breakfast-car express around 1930. (Dr Ian C. Allen/ Transport Treasury)

bogie wheel springing arrangements at Swindon and it was discovered that it only needed the track to be very slightly uneven (little more than an inch out) for the bogie wheels to leave the rails. The separate plate springs for the bogie wheels were clearly insufficiently robust to keep the bogie wheels on the track. Furthermore, the combination of minor track faults and engine rolling was putting excessive pressure on the springs, resulting in these breaking and the axle boxes running hot. Consequently, modifications to the bogie springing arrangements were immediately carried out on Nos 6001–6005. This involved the fitting of open wound coil springs at the ends of the plate springs, and changes to the axle boxes of the trailing bogie wheels to remove sideplay. In the event, this turned out to be only a temporary remedy, as described later.

Below right: No. 6004 keeps company with 'Saint' class No. 2978 Kirkland at Swindon Works in August 1938. (Michael Bentley collection)

No. 6000's triumphant American adventure

Having undertaken minimal trial running following its completion, and with no problems having arisen, No. 6000 was dismantled for loading on to a ship at Cardiff on 2 August. The boiler had to be detached from the frames because there was no crane strong enough at the docks to lift the complete locomotive, the cab sides and roof also being removed to facilitate the process. It is testament to the faith which the GWR had in this pioneer of a new class that they were prepared to let the locomotive run in America after barely a month of operation in Britain. This contrasts with the situation involving two less than brand-new LMS locomotives which visited America some years later. No chances were taken and the locomotives which masqueraded as *Royal Scot* and *Coronation* were in fact exchanged with another member of their respective classes perceived to be in better condition (i.e. ex-works).

The Baltimore & Ohio centenary event, entitled the Fair of the Iron Horse, celebrated the history of the steam locomotive. The GWR scored a major publicity coup by being the only British railway company to be invited to participate and in fact it had two exhibits. In addition to No. 6000, the GWR also sent over, for static display, the reconstructed non-working broad gauge engine, *North Star*, which had hauled the GWR's first passenger train in 1838.

Collett's assistant, William Stanier, was responsible for the locomotives while they were in America and he was accompanied by four other GWR employees: a driver, a fireman and two fitters. No. 6000 and *North Star* set off from Cardiff for America on 3 August 1927, reaching Baltimore on 21 August.

On arrival in America, No. 6000 was taken to the B&O's workshops at Mount Clare for reassembly and preparation for the centenary event which opened on 24 September at Halethorpe, some seven miles from Baltimore. In addition to the static display, there was a daily cavalcade of old and new engines, with No. 6000, representing the country which produced the first steam locomotives, being given the honour of leading the other modern examples: two Canadian and three American. These were enormous, clanking machines emitting large amounts of smoke, contrasting with the handsome, clean-cut lines of the 'King', which glided along the track emitting hardly any smoke and, as a result, stealing the show.

In the light of the Midgham derailment Collett contacted Stanier warning him that No. 6000 must not undertake any main line running until it too had received the specified modifications to its bogie springing arrangements. These were carried out under Stanier's supervision in the B&O's workshops.

The centenary celebrations ended on 15 October and two days later, No. 6000 started its main line trips. In order to comply with American railroad legislation the engine had to carry a bell. This was mounted directly on the running plate above the front bufferbeam. Later, in the 1950s, it was raised to prevent it from hitting the centre lamp bracket. The bell was fitted with an arm on one side of the pivot to which was connected a cable running to the cab, enabling the driver to ring the bell if necessary. This mechanism was subsequently removed on the locomotive's return to Britain to eliminate the temptation of crews ringing it for fun and creating a nuisance (particularly since it sounded like a fire engine!). The bell was inscribed with the words: *Presented to locomotive King George V by the Baltimore & Ohio Railroad Company in commemoration of its centenary celebrations Sept. 24th–Oct.15th 1927*. Four souvenir medals were also presented, two intended to be secured to each of the cab sides above the number plates.

The locomotive, hauling a rake of seven twelve-wheeled, all-steel coaches weighing 543 tons and full of VIPs, set off on a journey totalling some 270 miles from Baltimore to Washington, and then to Philadelphia, returning to Baltimore on the following day (18 October).

Given the weight of the train (around 150 tons heavier than the 'Cornish Riviera Express' before the weight of the latter was reduced by 'slip' coaches),

Below: As No. 6000 King George V prepares to set off from Baltimore to Washington on 17 October 1927, the American spectators are probably saying 'Gee, what a tiny engine!' as they compare the 4-6-0 with their own massive monsters. To comply with American railroad requirements, the locomotive carries a warning bell and a Westinghouse brake pump, the latter being fitted before it left for America and removed immediately on its return. (Meccano Magazine)

Left: Fit for a king ten years earlier (the King of Afghanistan), No. 6005 King George II hurries towards Black Bridge, Whitnash, near Leamington Spa, in Summer 1938. (Gordon Coltas collection)

Adulation amid concerns

he GWR crew's unfamiliarity with the road and the different type of coal used, the engine performed magnificently, showing its smooth riding qualities and sure-footedness on the gradients. The engine was officially limited to a top speed of 65mph, mainly due to much of the railway being unfenced and the number of level crossings the main reasons for a warning bell having to be fitted). Consequently, there was some consternation on the part of the American officials present when No. 6000 reached around 75mph between Washington and Philadelphia, whereupon the driver was told to reduce speed! The unqualified success of the American visit enhanced the reputation of British mechanical engineering across the world and the GWR in particular, whose publicity department lost no opportunity to exploit, particularly since it diverted attention away from the Midgham derailment.

No. 6000 arrived back in Britain on 26 November 1927 and was sent to Swindon for immediate reassembly. The locomotive re-entered service on 12 December 1927 at Old Oak Common depot and resumed its normal duties on London–West Country expresses. When King Amanullah of Afghanistan, on a seven-month European tour, visited Swindon Works on 21 March 1928, there was only one engine deemed appropriate to haul the king's train from Paddington to Swindon – No. 6000, of course! Collett then took the king on a tour of the works, which included an inspection of the footplate of No. 6005 *King George II*.

Such was the interest in the 'King' class locomotives that, even before No. 6000 had returned to these shores, the GWR has started running 'King'-hauled special trains to Swindon Works so that visitors could see for themselves where these engines were being built. Such specials

were extremely well patronised, some 50,000 people travelling on them in the first six months alone.

As well as being able to see 'Kings' under construction at Swindon, passengers on these 'King'-hauled specials also experienced an exciting ride. This was particularly so on the second of these excursions when No. 6001 *King Edward II* covered the 77.25 miles from London to Swindon at an average speed of around 68mph, the journey taking only 68.5min. Considering that, at the time these specials started, there were only six 'Kings' in service (once No. 6000 had been re-assembled) and two were rostered to work the 'Cornish Riviera Express', there was clearly little in the way of spare capacity for the class until the next batch (Nos 6006–6019) was completed between February and July 1928. These locomotives were fitted from the start with the revised

Right: Pre-arranged visits by the public to Swindon Works continued through the 1930s and well into the post-war period (the author remembers going in the late 1950s/early '60s). On 1 September 1949, a group have gathered beside No. 6000 King George V, which is standing on Churchward's stationary test plant in 'A' Shop. By running the locomotive with its drawbar coupled to the machinery, it was possible to measure its pulling power at various speeds. (J.C. Flemons/Transport Treasury)

Right: With revised springing arrangements having been fitted from new on No. 6011 King James I, the front end is being checked in this view at Swindon station around 1928, following a local running-in turn. A bowler-hatted gentleman at ground level peers at the front bogie while a fitter does likewise from the platform. (Transport Treasury collection)

springing arrangements on the front bogie, which had been subsequently fitted to the first six of the class.

Swindon was still not entirely happy with the modifications to the bogie springing and further testing was carried out. This included the creation of a unique bogie frame with a slot in the front crossbeam designed to cool the bogie wheel axle boxes. This slotted bogie frame was initially fitted to No. 6004 *King George III* but ended up under several members of the class including Nos 6000 and 6024.

An extraordinary test was carried out on No. 6004 on 16 May 1928 which beggars belief. The engine, driven by Clem Crook and fired by G. Humphries, made four light engine trips between Swindon and Didcot to monitor the emperature of the bearings of the leading bogie axle boxes. Sensors were attached to the axle boxes on each side and a temperature indicator was placed n the running plate. Driver Crook ecorded the data neatly on the back f a postcard.

On the first trip to Didcot, maximum speeds of 85mph and 95mph n the outward and return journeys espectively were achieved and on the econd trip the maximum speeds were 0mph and 102mph respectively. The ighest temperature recorded was 176° ahrenheit on the first journey and 77°F on the second journey.

In order to record the temperature, drawing office staff (it is assumed that here were two) were perched on seats bove the front bufferbeam with their acks to the direction of travel.

In view of the absence of leg room, t seems that the observers must have ad to have sat cross-legged for each of he 23-mile trips and the accompanying photographs show one such man. For rials involving observers placed at the ront of locomotives it was usual to fit an ndicator shelter around the smokebox vhich provided protection from the lements and, more importantly, prevented the observers from falling on o the track. With a shelter in place, they vould face the front and could watch the ine ahead through porthole windows.

In the case of No. 6004's trips, unless he drawing office staff were somehow trapped into their positions, they were isking their lives for the company as vell enduring considerable discomfort vith their backs to the wind. Such a practice would be impossible in today's Health and Safety world.

The official outcome of No. 6004's rials that day is not known but it is easonable to assume that the amount f extra cooling to the bogie axle boxes provided by the slotted front crossbeam vas insufficient to justify making his modification standard for the vhole class, as no further examples vere produced.

At about this time, all the 'Kings' which had already been built were

fitted with more substantial coil springs to the leading bogie wheels. Alterations were also made to the springing arrangements on the trailing bogie wheels involving the insertion of several thin metal plates. These modifications were successful in overcoming pitching and rolling and the constant problem of fractured springs. As a result, the riding qualities were now superb and no more problems arose with the

'Kings'' front bogie assembly, until metal fatigue occurred in the 1950s.

It has already been mentioned that the 'Kings' had cylinders with a diameter measuring 16.25in. In fact only the first six engines (Nos. 6000–6005) were built with cylinders of this size and on 6 November 1927 comparative tests were carried out between No. 6002 *King William IV*, which was specially fitted with 16in diameter

Above: In readiness for his white-knuckle ride, our hero takes his place above the bufferbeam of No. 6004 King George III at Swindon, and has managed to stay on board upon reaching Didcot North Junction, despite travelling at speeds up to 102mph! (Adrian Vaughan collection)

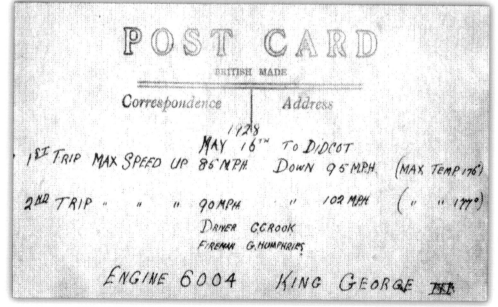

Left: A fascinating piece of history recorded on the back of a postcard! (Adrian Vaughan collection)

Right: In this picture, taken on 14 August 1959, the unique slotted bogie has been fitted to No. 6005 King George II, seen here about to stop at Knowle & Dorridge with the 5.10pm Paddington–Wolverhampton businessmen's train. (Michael Mensing)

Right: The way that trials with observers on the front of an engine was normally performed: No. 6005 King George II sports a protective indicator shelter at Swindon Works on 30 August 1931. (Michael Bentley collection)

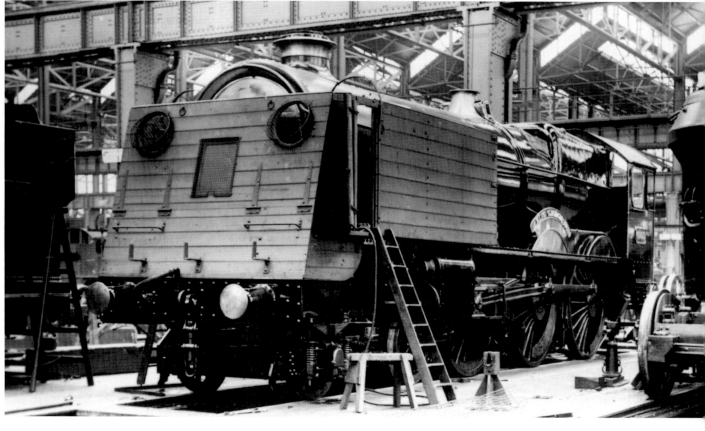

cylinders, and No. 6005 *King George II* with 16.25in cylinders.

The trials took place between Newton Abbot and Plymouth, i.e. over the South Devon banks, with each locomotive hauling a train of 13 empty carriages, the intention being to establish whether No. 6002, with its marginally smaller cylinders, was as strong as No. 6005. A further trial took place on 27 November just involving No. 6005. Although the tests showed that No. 6005, with its larger cylinders, had performed better on the banks than No. 6002, the decision was taken to reduce the cylinder size of the first batch of 'Kings' to 16in diameter and to fit this smaller size to the remainder of the class as they were built. However, subsequent re-borings on overhaul would increase the size closer to 16.25in and so this dimension continued to be used as the official figure for calculating the tractive effort, no doubt much to the relief of the GWR's Publicity Department!

Above: Here are photographs taken in later life of the engines used in the 1927 cylinder trials. The first shows No. 6002 King William IV backing out of Plymouth (Laira) shed before hauling the 'Cornishman' to Wolverhampton via Gloucester and Stratford-on-Avon. (Roy Vincent/Transport Treasury)

Left: The second is a mid-summer evening view (taken at 8.18pm) of the ubiquitous No. 6005 King George II, this time without slotted bogie or indicator shelter, thundering along between Widney Manor and Knowle & Dorridge with the 6.10pm Paddington–Birkenhead express on 28 June 1961. (Michael Mensing)

Operations extended

As stated previously, the 'Kings' entered service in the latter part of July 1927 on West of England trains, from Paddington via Westbury, working as far as Plymouth (North Road). They were also allowed to run to Bristol via Badminton, but it was well into 1928 before bridge strengthening had been completed at Bath to enable them to work on that route.

Although the initial requirement for the 'Kings' was to haul the heavy West Country summer holiday traffic, there was a similar need on the London to Birmingham line. In order to compete with the former London & North Western Railway direct route to Birmingham from Euston, the GWR, whose route from Paddington to Birmingham was originally via Didcot and Oxford, a distance of 129 miles, had built a new line from Old Oak Common to Aynho Junction, south of Banbury.

Almost half of the 73-mile length of the new line was jointly owned with the LNER (GC route) and once the final section from Princes Risborough to Aynho Junction (the 'Bicester Cut-off') was opened in 1910, the GWR was able to shorten the distance from Paddington to Birmingham Snow Hill to 110 miles, making this route three miles shorter than the LNWR's route from Euston to Birmingham New Street. The GWR was then able to advertise its express trains to Birmingham as taking the shortest route.

By the late 1920s, the GWR was running seven two-hour expresses each weekday, with a stop at Leamington Spa, with one train stopping at Princes Risborough instead. However, with some trains now weighing over 500 tons and the steep banks at Saunderton and Hatton to climb, this was a formidable task for 'Stars' and 'Castles'. Consequently, in the summer of 1928, three new 'Kings' (Nos 6017–6019) were sent to Wolverhampton (Stafford Road) shed to work this line, supplemented by Old Oak Common-based engines such as No. 6000, which had itself re-entered service on 12 December 1927.

Many trains on this route continued beyond Birmingham, to Wolverhampton,

Right: Entering the picture yet again, No. 6005 King George II takes water from Aynho troughs on 29 August 1962 when hauling the 5.10pm Paddington–Wolverhampton businessmen's train. A speed restriction caused by engineering works is making it hard to gather enough speed to scoop up water. (Michael Mensing)

This page: These three views depict 'Kings' on the London–Birmingham line in 1928, immediately after their introduction on this route. Above, No. 6000 King George V takes on water at Rowington troughs, between Lapworth and Hatton, while working what is probably the 2.35pm from Wolverhampton to Paddington, this being the regular return working of an Old Oak Common locomotive. Below is a view of No. 6017 King Edward IV near Bentley Heath and, finally left, back to No. 6000, King George V, also at Bentley Heath. (Author's collection; Michael Bentley collection)

Birkenhead, Shrewsbury and into Wales, but in the pre-war period weight restrictions prevented the 'Kings' from proceeding beyond Wolverhampton.

In the 1930s, consideration was given to reducing the two-hour schedule between Paddington and Birmingham to 1¾ hours to match the fastest times on the Paddington–Bristol route. However, the GWR's operating department insisted that the trains must weigh at least 300 tons tare (whereas the 'Bristolian' express weighed only 215 tons tare) and so the two-hour schedule remained the fastest time. With the 'Kings' in charge of the heaviest trains, reaching speeds in excess of 80mph they maintained the schedule while climbing the formidable hills with ease.

As mentioned earlier, 'King' haulage of the 'Cornish Riviera Express' started in 1927, as soon as they were introduced, but this was not the only titled train to be

Above and right: Two views taken in 1938. The first depicts No. 6006 King George I at Birmingham Snow Hill with the roundel device visible on its tender in place of the GWR coat of arms. The second shows photogenic No. 6005 King George II approaching Warwick with a down express. (George Barlow/ Transport Treasury; Gordon Coltas collection)

Left: Still in 1938 on the Birmingham line, No. 6025 King Henry III passes under Black Bridge, Whitnash, with an up train to London, and No. 6017 King Edward IV brings a down express into Leamington Spa. (Gordon Coltas collection)

worked by the class in the early days. In the following year, as more 'Kings' became available, they were introduced on the 'Torbay Limited' which linked London with Kingswear and, by way of the ferry, to the station without a railway at Dartmouth.

The 'Kings' enabled the 200 miles between Torquay and London to be undertaken in 3½ hours at an average speed of 57mph (60.4mph for the 164¾ miles between Exeter and Southall in West London, in line with the 'Cornish Riviera'). With the

strengthening of the bridges between Torquay and Kingswear, 'Kings' were able to haul the train for the entire journey.

On 8 July 1929 a Pullman train running two days a week between Paddington and Paignton was inaugurated, calling only

Below: A bird's eye view of Kingswear in the mid-1930s depicting No. 6023 King Edward II. (D.H. Bayes/Transport Treasury)

Right: No. 6010 King Charles I calls at Torquay station with the short-lived (1929–30) and arguably misnamed 'Torquay Pullman'. This train terminated at Paignton but presumably the GWR's publicity department regarded this as being a less attractive-sounding destination, probably because it was inland. (Author's collection)

requiring average speeds for the 118.3 miles to be maintained at 59.2mph travelling via Bath on the down working and 58.8mph for the slightly shorter Badminton route used for the up working. Trains running via Bath had slip portions for that destination labelled 'Bath Spa Express', providing a journey time from Paddington of 1.75 hours for the 107 miles.

At this point, reference should be made to some minor unique features on three early 'King' locomotives which were not perpetuated. No. 6004's slotted bogie frame has already been mentioned. No. 6001 was fitted with a small right-hand cabside window, seemingly to facilitate cleaning due to the obstruction caused by the automatic train control (ATC) apparatus inside the cab. Finally, No. 6000 was fitted with a small glass hinged window on the driver's side, apparently following its return from America, which it probably retained until all the cabside windows were removed and covered with steel for wartime blackout purposes.

In 1930, the final batch of 'Kings' emerged from Swindon Works, these

at Torquay and Newton Abbot. Initially composed of eight Pullman cars, the service was reduced to five carriages due to lack of patronage in 1930, and it was withdrawn completely at the end of that summer, never to run again. However, two of the 1928-built carriages, *Ione* and *Zena*, are still running on the main line today as part of the 'Venice Simplon Orient Express' (VSOE) rake.

'Kings' were also introduced on the London–Bristol two-hour expresses,

Right: No. 6000's unique small glass hinged window on the driver's side is clearly visible in this photograph taken at Leamington Spa, some time before May 1934 when the GWR coat of arms on this locomotive's tender was replaced by the roundel motif. (Gordon Coltas collection)

being Nos 6020 to 6029. They differed from the two previous batches by being built with the smokebox step with which all members of the class were later disfigured until the early 1950s. In addition, the final ten locomotives were built with modified inside valve covers and top feed pipes which curved round behind the nameplate rather than going vertically all the way down the boiler. The 20 earlier engines were modified accordingly to match the new machines.

The last engine in the final batch was completed in August 1930 and represented the GWR (along with the reconstructed *North Star*) at the Liverpool & Manchester Railway centenary celebrations held in the following month (13–20 September). No. 6029 was serviced at Agecroft shed and then went on display at Wavertree Playground, Liverpool, where a railway link connected to the Liverpool to Crewe line had been specially installed for the occasion.

Above: One is left to speculate whether it was by design or sheer coincidence that, at the Liverpool Exhibition in 1930, No. 6029 King Stephen stood immediately in front of a 'Lord Nelson' 4-6-0, serving as a reminder to the Southern Railway that this class was no longer the most powerful passenger locomotive type, following the arrival of the GWR 'Kings'! (Great Western Trust collection)

Left: No. 6000 King George V passes through Wellington, Somerset, near the border with Devon, in about 1930. With Whiteball Tunnel at the top, Wellington Bank rises to 1 in 80, down which City of Truro achieved its 102.3mph speed record in 1904. (Author's collection)

GWR publicity using the 'Kings'

The GWR was always very publicity-conscious and wasted no time in extolling the virtues of the new 'King' class and ensuring that these engines featured prominently in their promotional material such as posters, jigsaws and books. The very naming of its most powerful locomotives after kings and ensuring that the first of the class was named in honour of the reigning monarch of the time was an inspired choice. The subsequent re-namings of two members of the class to reflect the next two new monarchs, at the expense of the two earliest ones, was another example of the GWR's publicity machine not missing a trick.

Right and below: The boxes of the 150-piece and 300-piece jig-saw puzzles depicting No. 6000 King George V. (Author's collection)

Like other 'Big Four' railway companies, the GWR produced some iconic posters in

the period before the Second World War, with some of the most notable featuring 'Kings', for example, hauling an express past the sea wall between Dawlish and Teignmouth in Devon, or advertising 'Speed to the West'.

The GWR was also a prolific producer of jigsaw puzzles, producing 44 different images in the 1920s and 1930s, most of them depicting tourist places served by the railway, but a few were of actual trains and, in a couple of cases, particular classes of locomotive. The first puzzle, produced in 1924, featured the pioneer 'Castle' class locomotive, No. 4073 *Caerphilly Castle*. Unsurprisingly, the puzzle was withdrawn

in 1928 because 'Castle' class locomotives were now playing second fiddle to the 'King' class and a jigsaw puzzle depicting No. 6000 *King George V* (based on its official photograph taken before the engine received its bell), was issued in 1927. This comprised some 150 pieces and was followed shortly after by one with more than 300 pieces.

In addition, the GWR produced guide books aimed at holidaymakers as well as more esoteric ones for railway enthusiasts. Several of these latter books featured images of 'Kings' on their covers and this remained the case, in terms of books, jigsaw puzzles and posters, right up to the Second World War. The reason for this was that in the 1930s (indeed up to the introduction of diesel-hydraulics in 1958), express locomotive development on the GWR had not advanced since 1927 so there had been nothing to replace the 'Kings' with regard to publicising the company's fast and powerful locomotives.

There was no equivalent of the LNER's 'Silver Jubilee' express hauled by streamlined A4 Pacifics or the LMS's 'Coronation Scot' train hauled by equally distinctive streamlined 'Duchesses'. The GWR was getting left behind in terms of express locomotive development although it could be argued that the GWR's main publicity drive was to attract holidaymakers to the West Country

Below: The completed 150-piece jigsaw puzzle depicts No. 6000 in its as-built condition, without its bell and commemorative cabside-mounted medallions. The image shows the original bogie springing arrangement, vertical top feed pipes, and inside valve cover design. (Author's collection)

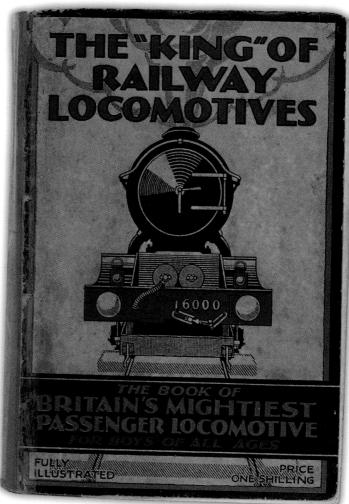

Left: 'Kings' depicted on the covers of The 'King' of Railway Locomotives published in 1928 and The GWR Engine Book published in 1932. (Author's collection)

where its only competitor was therefore the Southern Railway, over whose express engines the GWR undoubtedly had the edge before the emergence of Bulleid's locomotives in the 1940s.

Portraits of 'Kings' also appeared on other GWR-produced material such as menu cards, which patrons were allowed to take away with them, and working models of 'King' locomotives in glass cases were located on some stations. On visits to Paddington station as a boy in the 1950s, the author recalls always asking his mother for a coin to insert into the case displaying a model of a 'King' in order to activate the locomotive's wheels and motion.

In the immediate post-war period, BR

Western Region experimented with two gas-turbine locomotives but, on the basis of their overall performance, they were inferior to the 'Kings'. So these latter, by then somewhat elderly engines, remained the ultimate express passenger locomotive on the Western Region and continued to feature in publicity. The author has a BR timetable for train services between Machynlleth and Pwllheli in Summer 1960, and this features an image of a 'King', largely based on the iconic pre-war 'Speed to the West' painting (but with the Centenary stock behind the engine changed to standard stock). It is amazing that, at this time of unrelenting dieselisation, BR was using a 33-year-old locomotive type for promotion purposes.

TRAIN SERVICES AND CHEAP FARE FACILITIES

between

ABERYSTWYTH, DEVIL'S BRIDGE, MACHYNLLETH, ABERDOVEY, TOWYN, BARMOUTH, HARLECH, PORTMADOC, CRICCIETH, PENYCHAIN, PWLLHELI and intermediate Stations

13th JUNE to 11th SEPTEMBER inclusive, 1960

BRITISH RAILWAYS

Left: The author seldom retained railway timetables during his childhood, but resolved to keep this one depicting a 'King' because of his astonishment that the Western Region was still using the image at this time, of a 33-year-old locomotive type. (Author's collection)

1931–1945
Through the Thirties and the Second World War

When Nos 6000–6005 were built, their tenders carried the garter coat of arms flanked by the words 'Great Western'. On the 'Kings', this crest was superseded by the GWR coat of arms in 1929, which in turn was replaced by the roundel motif, with no lettering, introduced in 1934.

The 'Kings' had been named in descending chronological order, so that *King Stephen* (No. 6029) was the 29th male monarch to precede *King George V*. When the king died, the GWR decided to rename No. 6029 in May 1936 after his successor and eldest son, *King Edward VIII*.

The company, like the rest of the nation, was unprepared for the king's abdication prior to his coronation and hastily changed the name of No. 6028 from *King Henry II* to that of the new monarch, *King George VI*, in January 1937, thus breaking the chronological order of the class names. Bearing in mind that during 1936, no fewer than three kings reigned in Britain, the GWR did well to keep up with these changes, and reflect them in the naming of its 'King' class locomotives.

BUCKINGHAM PALACE

22nd. December, 1936.

My dear Horne,

Thank you for your two letters of December 18th.

I have conveyed to The King and Queen your good wishes, which were much appreciated, and the formal resolution from the Great Western Railway has been forwarded to the Home Office, from whom in due course you will receive a reply.

With regard to your request that you should be allowed to call one of your latest types of locomotive engines after King George VI, His Majesty is very pleased to grant permission for this to be done.

Yours sincerely,

Wigram

The Right Honble.
    Sir Robert Horne,
        GBE.,
    Great Western Railway,
        Board Room,
            Paddington Station, W.2.

Above: King George VI was proclaimed King on 12 December 1936 and the GWR wasted no time in writing to Buckingham Palace for permission to name one of their "latest types of locomotive engines" (in fact a ten year old design!) after the new King, which was immediately granted. (National Archives)

Left and above left: No. 6029 stands at Bristol Bath Road shed on 10 November 1935 bearing its King Stephen nameplates. Less than 18 months later, the locomotive is pictured in Swindon shed on 18 April 1937 carrying its new identity, King Edward VIII, by which time the actual personage was no longer on the throne! (Michael Bentley collection)

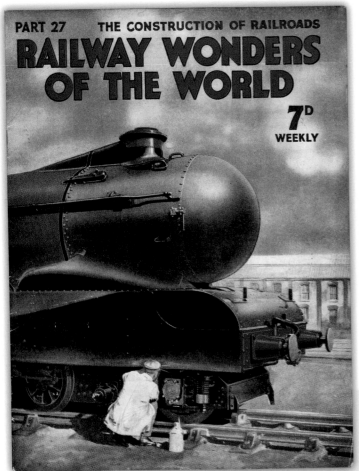

PART 27   THE CONSTRUCTION OF RAILROADS

RAILWAY WONDERS OF THE WORLD

7D WEEKLY

The 'King' with the bulbous nose

The centenary of the GWR was commemorated in 1935 and the Board decided that it would be appropriate to show off the company's modernising credentials by embracing streamlining, a concept developed by some overseas railway companies for reducing air resistance and increasing speeds. Collett appeared to be less than enthusiastic about the idea and made what some people consider to be a half-hearted attempt to placate the Board by designing something so hideous and impractical that it was almost guaranteed to result in the scheme being abandoned. On the other hand, it is important to remember that Collett's experiment at streamlining pre-dated the LNER's A4 class by several months and the LMS's 'Princess Coronations' by two years, so he was largely out on his own as regards streamlining in Britain. Furthermore, he was adapting an existing design rather than creating a new class. His source of inspiration was hardly 'high-tech' though – he simply applied some Plasticine to a paperweight model of a 'King' and sent it to the drawing office!

Collett chose two victims for his experiment: No. 6014 *King Henry VII* and 'Castle' class No. 5005 *Manorbier Castle*.

The unlucky 'King' entered service in March 1935, but the result of high-speed trials showed no appreciable difference in performance from the rest of the class, and the shroudings around the cylinders tended to cause overheating of the motion, as well as making maintenance more difficult.

In August 1935, the fairings around the cylinders, steam pipes and on the tender were removed and from then on other bits of streamlining gradually disappeared, the bulbous nose being

Above: Pity the driver attempting to oil up No. 6014 King Henry VII with all that paraphernalia getting in the way! (Railway Wonders of the World)

Right: Nice location, shame about the engine! No. 6014 King Henry VII approaches Dawlish with an up express from the West Country in Summer 1935. (Dr Ian C. Allan/ Transport Treasury)

discarded in December 1942. The straight splashers and nameplate reverted to the original rounded design in October 1944. However, two features were perpetuated elsewhere. No. 6014 was fitted with a cab roof sliding ventilator and eventually, from 1954, the remainder of the class were so treated, while the straight splashers and nameplates became a striking feature of the Hawksworth 'County' class 4-6-0s introduced in 1945.

No. 6014 remained unique until its withdrawal, in two respects: the wedge-shaped cab was retained, as was the special bracket fitted to the inside steam chest cover for attaching train reporting numbers (because such a bracket could not be fitted to the bulbous nose). This locomotive therefore became the only 'King' to run without its BR smokebox number plate being obscured by a train reporting number.

Above: No. 6014 displays the absence of fairings round the cylinders and steam pipes as it stands at Birmingham Snow Hill station on 17 May 1936. (J.A. Whaley/Transport Treasury)

Left: With its uniquely positioned train reporting number, former semi-streamliner No. 6014 coasts round the curve through Priestfield station, near Wolverhampton, with the 2.10pm Paddington–Birkenhead train on 30 April 1960. (Michael Mensing)

Celebration of the GWR's centenary in 1935

Although the first section of the GWR, from London to Maidenhead, was not opened to the public until 4 June 1838, the centenary of the railway was taken to be 100 years from 31 August 1835. This was the date when Royal Assent was given to the Bill authorising the construction of the line between London and Bristol.

The GWR marked its centenary in 1935 in several ways. As stated earlier, one development introduced as part of the celebrations was the semi-streamlining of two unfortunate locomotives. Another was the building of new carriages, known as Centenary Stock, for its most prestigious train, the 'King'-hauled 'Cornish Riviera Express'.

These distinctive coaches were built to the maximum possible width of 9ft 7in, having recessed doors to prevent the handles from protruding. A single example survives today: one of two first class kitchen restaurant cars. Owned by the Great Western Society, it is on display at Didcot Railway Centre.

The centenary was also commemorated by the introduction of a new titled train to emphasis the company's origins – the linking of London and Bristol as evidenced in the GWR's crest, which displays the coats of arms of the two cities. The new train was named the 'Bristolian' and used 'King' class locomotives, at least initially and at other times during its subsequent operation. As a precursor to the new train, on 31 August 1935, the official centenary date, a special train carrying directors and invited guests travelled from Paddington to Bristol, where various celebrations were held, during which an announcement was made about the new train and the fact that it would clip 15 minutes off the normal two-hour schedule. The special then returned to London, completing the journey in 105min 29sec, slightly disappointing perhaps but nevertheless demonstrating that the new 105min schedule was realistic. Not surprisingly, the special was hauled by the company's flagship locomotive, No. 6000 *King George V*.

Nine days later, the 'Bristolian' was inaugurated, covering the 118-mile distance between the two cities in 105min at an average speed of 67mph. Contemporaneous reports indicate that the 'Kings' were easily capable of sustained high-speed running on this train, with 90 miles being covered at speeds consistently in excess of over 70mph, but without the need to exceed 80mph, in order to maintain the 105min schedule under normal conditions. However, the 'Kings' could achieve speeds up to 95mph to bring the 'Bristolian' to its destination on time if delays due to signal checks and permanent way restrictions had been experienced en route. Nevertheless, the 'Kings' were not designed to haul lightweight high-speed trains such as this. On the other hand, 'Castles' were able to demonstrate their suitability for this type of service as a result of their exploits on the 'Cheltenham Flyer' and consequently 'Castles' became the more usual motive power for the 'Bristolian' rather than the 'Kings'.

Right: The 'King'-hauled 'Cornish Rivera Express' composed of wide-bodied 'Centenary' stock. The only survivor from this stock, Centenary Dining Car No. 9635, is preserved at the Didcot Railway Centre.
(Meccano Magazine)

Below: The GWR 'Centenary Special' near Badminton on its journey from Paddington to Bristol on 31 August 1935, hauled by No. 6000 King George V.
(W. Vaughan-Jenkins/ Meccano Magazine)

Fallen majesties

'King' class locomotives were unfortunate to be involved in two major train crashes which resulted in fatalities, although neither was caused by any engine defect.

The first of these accidents occurred at around 5am on 15 January 1936 at Shrivenham in Wiltshire, and involved No. 6007 *King William III* hauling a Penzance to Paddington sleeper. A faulty coupling on a preceding coal train from Aberdare to Old Oak Common hauled by 2-8-0 freight locomotive No. 2802 caused the train to split, leaving five wagons and the brake van on the up main line. The signalmen at both Shrivenham and Ashbury Crossing failed to notice that there was no red lamp showing at the end of the train as it passed by. The express was given a clear road and ploughed into the stationary wagons, killing the driver and one passenger. The freight train's guard survived unscathed as he had alighted from the brakevan when it had come to an unexpected halt.

No. 6007 was taken back to Swindon Works and, as a result of the extent and cost of the necessary repairs, which exceeded that of a normal overhaul, a new Lot number was issued and, for

TRAIN WRECK
Penzance-London express crashed into runaway goods trucks at Shrivenham, Berks, January 15. Two killed, 23 injured. One of the dead was 51-year-old driver, E. Starr. As he lay trapped in wreckage, he advised rescuers how to work, smiled to the end.

Above: No. 6007 King William III lies on its side at Shrivenham on 15 January 1936. One carriage has rammed into the locomotive's cab while another has overturned. Tragically, there were two fatalities, including the driver. (Shrivenham Heritage Centre collection)

Left: Looking in fine shape 25 years after its rebuild, No. 6007 King William III pulls away from Leamington Spa in May 1961 with an up express to London. (Alan Sainty collection)

Right: One of the whistle covers from No. 6028 which was found by a schoolboy in a field adjacent to the Norton Fitzwarren crash site. (Great Western Trust collection)

conclude that an entirely new locomotive was constructed but, as can be seen from the accompanying photograph, the engine was certainly not destroyed. Many parts were re-used including major items such as the frames, boiler and tender, and No. 6007 re-entered service on 24 March 1936, just over two months after the train crash, having cost £4,393 to rebuild.

The second accident occurred near Norton Fitzwarren in Somerset on 4 November 1940 and involved No. 6028 *King George VI*, an unfortunate casualty considering this engine was the one carrying the name of the reigning monarch at that time. It was also a very serious accident in terms of loss of life, with 26 persons being killed, including the fireman, but ironically, not the driver who was held responsible for the crash, albeit under some mitigating circumstances, including the fact that his house had just been bombed.

The train was the 9.50pm from Paddington to Penzance and when it left Taunton station, the driver erroneously thought he was on the Down Main line when he was in fact on the parallel Down Relief line. He thought that the favourable signal he was passing applied to him and therefore ignored the warning sounds from the Automatic Train Control system informing him that he was passing a danger signal.

The driver's statement at the subsequent enquiry that he had been signalled to take the Down Main was not accepted but some six years later the signalman admitted privately that he had momentarily signalled the express to take the Down Main before changing his mind and giving clearance instead to a newspaper train. One can imagine the express driver's horror when he found himself being overtaken by the other train. At this point it was too late to stop and the express, now travelling at around 45mph went through the catch points where the two tracks merged, and the locomotive and the first five carriages overturned.

As with No. 6007, No. 6028 was taken to Swindon Works and repaired very quickly, the work being less substantial with this locomotive and not regarded as a replacement build. The locomotive re-entered service on 21 February 1941.

accounting purposes, the locomotive was officially condemned on 5 March 1936 (i.e. the company's asset was written off). This seems to have caused some people to

Right: Like No. 6007, No. 6028 King George VI was quickly put back into service after its accident. In its last year of operation it is seen hauling the up 'Red Dragon' through Ealing Broadway station on 17 March 1962, just before 'Hymek' diesels took over. (Great Western Trust collection)

For king and country

The 'Kings' had a largely uneventful war, apart from the disastrous train crash at Norton Fitzwarren in 1940 described in the previous section. Cleanliness was of course sacrificed, but otherwise their external appearance remained unchanged except for the fitting of steel in place of the cabside windows for black-out purposes, and their livery being changed to unlined green. At least they were spared the indignity of being painted black like some other companies' top-link locomotives. On 1 September 1939, two days before war was declared, the railway companies were put under Government control and express train schedules were slowed down in order to concentrate on essential wartime traffic. This consisted initially of evacuation trains taking children from the cities to the countryside. It was not long before Swindon Works had to contribute to the war effort by making armaments and locomotive overhauls were necessarily reduced. With the best coal being supplied to shipping, the quality of locomotive coal worsened, a situation which, due to the absence of large superheaters, had a particularly adverse effect on GWR express locomotives.

After the evacuation trains ceased, the emphasis switched to the movement of military personnel and a number of 'Kings' were transferred to West Country depots. For example, No. 6000 *King George V*, which had been shedded at Old Oak Common since June 1927 (apart from its sojourn in America), found itself allocated to Newton Abbot in October 1939, before moving to Exeter the following month.

Trains carrying so many service personnel were frequently overloaded, but the 360 tons limit for 'Kings' over the Devon banks remained, heavier trains still requiring piloting. As the war progressed and maximum utilisation of locomotives became essential, the Devon-based 'Kings' hauling trains into London

Below: Before being transferred to Exeter shed in November 1939, No. 6000 King George V was a regular visitor to the area, hauling trains to and from the West Country. In this view dating from the start of the 1930s, the locomotive brings a down express into Exeter St David's station. (Michael Bentley collection)

could find themselves used on a return Wolverhampton line working before returning to the West Country. Yet, despite more intensive operating, poorer quality coal and reduced servicing frequencies, the 'Kings' soldiered on through the war capably.

The London–Birmingham line also witnessed packed trains during the war years, with 'Kings' regularly hauling loads between 475 and 545 tons unaided up Hatton bank where, for 2 miles, the gradient varies between 1 in 110 to 1 in 103.

Plymouth was a particular target for enemy bombers, not so much for its railway installations, but for its dockyard (Devonport). At the height of the blitz, locomotives shedded at Plymouth (Laira) were evacuated to the Cornwall side of the River Tamar, special dispensation being given for 'Kings' to travel individually at very low speed across the Royal Albert Bridge, over which they were normally banned at this time.

One member of the class, No. 6010 *King Charles I*, had a lucky escape from being

Above: Hatton Bank has always been a challenge for heavy trains (as well as for boats on the neighbouring Grand Union Canal, where there are 21 locks in a stretch of less than two miles). No. 6015 King Richard III storms up the incline on 11 March 1956 with the 11.10am Paddington–Birkenhead express. (Michael Mensing)

Right: The 'King' with the shortest name, No. 6026 King John, rests at Plymouth (Laira) shed in the company of auto-fitted small Prairie tank No. 5572, now preserved at Didcot. (Roy Vincent/ Transport Treasury)

Left: Lucky to escape destruction and long since devoid of its bullet holes, No. 6010 King Charles I presents a stirring sight as it heads the 9.10am Paddington–Birkenhead express near Knowle & Dorridge on 13 October 1956. (Michael Mensing)

badly damaged or destroyed at Newton Abbot. In the evening of 20 August 1940, enemy aircraft (two bombers and a fighter) attacked the station and depot. Six bombs were dropped but only five exploded. The sixth struck a rail which caused it to slide off at an angle, coming to rest on its side just two roads away from where the 'King' was standing, fortunately failing to explode. One of the remaining bombs exploded only some 40 feet away from No. 6010, causing it slight damage. However, worse was to follow. Once the bombers had finished their business the fighter aircraft straffed the whole area with machine gun fire. The 'King' was hit several times, the tender being riddled with holes, and the driver and fireman were badly injured. In all, 14 people were killed in this attack on the station and depot, four of whom were GWR employees, and 15 others were seriously injured.

Unofficial photography of railway activity during the Second World War was not permitted. Even official photographs

were few and far between, apart from those recording the results of enemy action, but occasionally, happier events such as the one featured here were recorded.

On a more frivolous wartime note, the appearance of one member of the class

changed for a time in 1943 – No. 6000 *King George V* had to run without its bell because it went missing! According to one story, some American serviceman who had a stores depot within the Swindon Works complex took a fancy to the bell because

Left: There was Turkish delight for a group of engineers on 24 February 1943 when, on a visit to England, they were invited to Swindon Works and were photographed aboard No. 6026 King John, which was decorated for the occasion with the Union and Turkish flags. (The Railway Magazine)

it reminded them of home. Consequently, they decided to steal the bell and it ended up mounted on the front of a Sherman tank on active service in France. Following a tip-off, the bell was later found in the Serpentine in Hyde Park (or a lake in Berkshire, according to another version of the story), and returned to the GWR. In the meantime, Swindon had cast a replica bell in accordance with drawing No. 119675, which was described as 'Bell for engine No. 6000 *King George V*, Swindon, July 1943'. This one was reputedly slightly more yellow than the original which was more of a copper colour. The replica bell, which had been carried by the locomotive, was then replaced by the original one.

There is an alternative version of the story of the missing bell, namely that it was stolen by Welsh apprentices at Swindon Works. They had seen No. 6000 standing outside A Shop awaiting repair and decided, probably when they were the worse for drink, that it would be suitable as a breakfast bell in their lodgings in the Toc H in Old Swindon. At this stage, they did not realise that it would never have been effective because it no longer had a clapper! Back at the works, two of the apprentices took the opportunity of studying the mounting of the bell and found that it was held by only one nut. They hid a spanner on the engine and returned at night to undo the nut and remove the bell. However, the bell did not come free and they did not risk forcing it for fear of making too much noise. Replacing the fixing nut hand tight, the apprentices returned the following night with a metal bar to prise off the bell which fell from its mounting and hit the bufferbeam, making a tremendous racket. Surprisingly, no one appeared, so they wrapped the bell in a sack and took it to the boundary fence. It was lifted over the following day and taken to the Toc H, whereupon it was found to be useless for the intended purpose. The bell was then taken home by one of the apprentices and secreted under his bed. This apprentice subsequently got married and, due to the housing shortage, moved in temporarily

with his new in-laws, bringing the bell with him. It was then stored for some three years in the cupboard under the stairs, after which it was somehow returned to the GWR.

Even if the original bell had not been stolen, it would have been sensible for the GWR to cast a second bell as a contingency measure. The gold medallions awarded by the Baltimore & Ohio Railroad had already been replicated as soon as the locomotive returned to Swindon from its American visit, these replicas being placed in brass-rimmed frames attached to the cab sides.

Another wartime story, but one over which there is uncertainty as to whether it is fact or fiction, concerns the design of a 'Super King'. In the latter stages of the war, with Hawksworth more receptive to new ideas than Collett, his predecessor, and with a desire emerging at Swindon to prepare for a return to faster schedules at the end of hostilities, there appears to

have been some consideration given to producing a Pacific. Some preliminary design work is believed to have been carried out before the project, which was being undertaken somewhat surreptitiously, was quietly dropped. This decision was hardly surprising, in light of the weight restrictions which bedevilled *The Great Bear* and, as No. 6018 ably demonstrated as it climbed out of King's Cross station in 1948, the better adhesion abilities of 4-6-0s over 4-6-2s, this being essential for taking heavy trains up the Dainton, Rattery and Hemerdon banks in the West Country. However, it seems that some of the 'Super King' ideas were adopted for the 4-6-0 'Counties' such as 6ft 3in driving wheels and 280lb boiler pressure, and these locomotives did perform well over the South Devon banks. It should be emphasised, however, that there is a body of opinion which considers that the plans for a Hawksworth Pacific are a myth.

Opposite: Re-united with its bell, No. 6000 King George V waits at Plymouth (Laira) shed on 23 July 1953 before hauling the 'Cornish Riviera Express' to Paddington. The bell was later mounted on a small wooden plinth so that, if swung, it no longer hit the centre lamp bracket. The original tapered buffers, as seen here, were replaced on the entire class with parallel ones. (Geoff Rixon)

Below: The pride of Old Oak Common, No. 6000 King George V, displays its replica gold medallions as it rests inside the shed on 30 September 1962, the day after hauling the Talyllyn special to Ruabon (one way) and then piloting an ailing diesel on the return journey. (Geoff Rixon)

1946–1961
Decline and revival

The GWR, along with the other main line railway companies, was in a parlous state by the end of the Second World War, following six years of make do and mend. Locomotive maintenance had necessarily been kept to a minimum and a shortage of labour meant that non-essential activities such as cleaning engines had to be curtailed. This remained the case in the early post-war period, as evidenced by contemporary photographs showing unkempt 'Kings'.

Right: Carrying a 'Not to be moved' sign, No. 6008 King James II awaits attention at Wolverhampton (Stafford Road) in June 1946. (Graham Ellis/Transport Treasury)

Far left: Vestiges of outward respectability are evident in this view of No. 6012 King Edward VI photographed at Woodborough, Wiltshire, in 1948. (Michael Bentley collection)

Left and below: The empty reporting number frames festooned across the smokebox add to the general scruffiness portrayed by No. 6005 King George II at Olton in December 1948, and No. 6008 King James II, now back on the move, at Warwick on 10 September 1949. (J.C. Flemons/ Transport Treasury; Neil Davenport)

Post-war blues and initial modifications

Below: Probably on its final day of service, No. 6022 King Edward III pulls out of Wolverhampton Low Level on 8 September 1962, the date marking the end of scheduled 'King' operation on BR. (John McCann/Online Transport Archive)

As stated in the previous chapter, towards the end of the Second World War as victory looked more likely, the GWR started preparing for the end of hostilities, with the expectation that in due course, timings of express passenger services would be accelerated and that trains would become heavier. By this time, Collett had been succeeded by Hawksworth who was convinced that increased superheating would improve performance. Churchward's policy, which was continued by Collett, was that the higher superheating being implemented on other railways was unnecessary and all that was required was low-temperature superheating sufficient to ensure that, at the end of the expansion in the cylinders, the steam temperature would be just above saturation point. This was a reasonable principle when Welsh coal with its high calorific value was used, but its availability was no longer guaranteed and higher temperature superheating was needed. Consequently, a new three-row superheater was designed and fitted to the 'Modified Hall' class introduced in 1944, and to the new batch of 'Castles' which followed

two years later. Following on from these developments, No. 6022 *King Edward III* received a new four-row superheater boiler in late 1947.

However, while No. 6022's capabilities were still being assessed, the GWR ceased to exist, being replaced by BR Western Region. This was a consequence of nationalisation which occurred on 1 January 1948 and within a couple of months it was decided to instigate some locomotive exchanges across the regions. This was ostensibly to identify best locomotive design practice from within

the four old companies, which could be used for the proposed new BR Standard designs. Three ex-GWR locomotives were trialled on other lines: No. 6990 *Witherslack Hall* on the former Great Central main line (and now preserved on that line), and No. 3803 (also preserved, this time on the South Devon Railway), which was used on freight trials and, crucially, No. 6018 *King Henry VI* on the East Coast Main Line between King's Cross and Leeds.

The Western Region might have been expected to have used its flagship locomotive, No. 6000 *King George V* for an important event such as these Interchange Trials (the Eastern Region produced *Mallard*

Left: No. 6018 King Henry VI, which represented the Western Region in the 1948 Locomotive Exchanges, is on home territory at Iver, Buckinghamshire, hauling the down 'Merchant Venturer' to Weston-super-Mare on 20 July 1951. (J.C. Flemons/ Transport Treasury)

amongst other A4s), but No. 6000 was due for a heavy general repair, having run up a high mileage since its previous overhaul. Besides, the Western Region was less than enthusiastic about these trials, perhaps anticipating that its express passenger locomotive development would be judged as having stagnated.

Despite being 4-6-0s, BR classified the 'Kings' as 8P, in company with the 4-6-2s of the other former companies (the Southern's 'Merchant Navy' class, the LMS's 'Princess Royal' and 'Coronation' ('Duchess') classes, and the Eastern's A4s). Along with the LMS 7P rebuilt 'Royal Scot' class, these locomotives were pitched against the 'King'.

The main series of trials started on

home territory, with No. 6018 working between Paddington and Plymouth from 20 to 23 April before transferring to the Eastern Region to run trials between King's Cross and Leeds from 18 to 21 May. However, in order to create the proverbial level playing field, Yorkshire 'hard' coal instead of Welsh 'soft' coal, to which the 'Kings' were accustomed, had to be used on both regions. A combination of circumstances, including the type of coal and the leisurely schedule (compared with pre-war timings) resulted in an unspectacular performance from No. 6018, although the locomotive impressed with its surefootedness, climbing out of King's Cross station.

The GWR, being vehemently opposed

to nationalisation, ensured that the locomotives which it was using for these trials, stubbornly wore GWR livery (the coat of arms flanked by the letters G and W) and still carried the front number on the bufferbeam. Because of clearance difficulties, the 'King' was only allowed to run on the Eastern Region, and not on the Southern or London Midland Regions. Arguably, this put it at a disadvantage compared with the other regions' express passenger locomotives, which were able to travel more widely and therefore provided an opportunity to achieve a more balanced result, although it must be said that No. 6018's trials on the Western Region, where it should have excelled, were not particularly impressive either.

Above left: Making a preliminary run on 10 May 1948, No. 6018 King Henry VI approaches Wood Green with the 1.10pm from King's Cross to Leeds. (Graham Ellis/ Transport Treasury)

Above right: With Churchward's ancient dynamometer car (now preserved) coupled behind the engine, No. 6018 storms through Potters Bar Cutting at the head of one of the test trains, again the 1.10pm King's Cross–Leeds, on 18 May 1948. (Graham Ellis/ Transport Treasury)

Right: Both trialled engines seen in later life: No. 6001 King Edward VII passes a Central Line tube train as it approaches Mason's Green Lane overbridge at Park Royal at the head of a Birmingham express on 24 March 1961. (Bruce Jenkins)

Right: The high superheat guinea-pig, No. 6022 King Edward III, having restarted the 5.10pm Paddington–Wolverhampton businessmen's train at Knowle & Dorridge, approaches the level crossing at Bentley Heath on 5 July 1961. (Michael Mensing)

Opposite: Here is another view of one of the trialled locomotives, No. 6001. King Edward VII, pounding its way through the open landscape between Windney Manor and Knowle and Dorridge with the 8.05am Birkenhead-Paddington express on Sunday 21 December 1958. (Michael Mensing)

There was particular concern about No. 6018's coal consumption figures in the trials. On its home ground, the engine achieved an average of only 3.74lb of coal per drawbar horsepower hour (dhp hr), worse than any of the 'foreign' locomotives. The best results on the Paddington–Plymouth runs were from the A4 (3.19lb per dhp hr) and the 'Duchess' (3.24lb per dhp hr). No. 6018 fared better on the King's Cross–Leeds runs (3.39lb per dhp hr), coming second worst in front of the 'Merchant Navy' (3.73lb per dhp hr). Nevertheless, overall, No. 6018's results were disappointing and on the basis that, in its early life, No. 6005 *King George II* had been put under test with Welsh coal and achieved 3lb per dhp hr, Swindon considered the April/May 1948 trials involving the use of Yorkshire coal as unfair (the brand-new 'Modified Hall' with its three-row superheater also turned in poor coal consumption figures).

Following representations made by the Western Region, it was agreed that further tests could take place on the Paddington–Plymouth line, this time using Welsh coal. The supplementary trials were conducted from 23 to 26 November 1948 using a standard 'King' (No. 6001 *King Edward VII*) and for the period 14–17 December 1948, using the high-superheated example (No. 6022 *King Edward III*).

No. 6001 showed a slight improvement in performance (3.33lb per dhp hr, although allowing for the higher calorific value of the Welsh coal compared with the Yorkshire coal, the equivalent value was 3.5lb – not greatly better than the original 3.74lb). However, No. 6022 with its four-row superheater boiler produced a much better result (3.1lb or 3.25lb when adjusted for calorific value).

There was frustration in Western Region circles that No. 6018 had not emulated the fine performance of No. 4079 *Pendennis Castle* on the LNER in the 1925 exchange trials, when Yorkshire coal was also used. However, it must be remembered that, at the time, No. 4079 was a new locomotive whereas No. 6018 was almost 20 years old and the original design had not been updated. The disappointing results were largely put down to the engine's low

superheating and, in hindsight, it seems unfortunate that the Western Region did not use its high-superheated example, No. 6022. At the time of the trials, it was already showing an improvement in performance as a result of this modification, although it had only recently re-entered service.

Another consequence of Nationalisation was a desire to have uniform 'corporate' colours to replace the various liveries used by the old companies. Different colour schemes were tried and a number of 8P locomotives, including eight 'Kings', the first being Nos 6009 and 6025, were painted dark (Prussian) blue with red, cream and grey lining, similar to the old Great Eastern Railway livery. By early 1949, it was decided to paint 8P locomotives in a

lighter (Caledonian Railway) blue with black and white lining. The entire 'King' class was so treated, No. 6000 *King George V* being the first to be painted in this livery, in June 1948.

The Caledonian-style blue livery was found not to weather particularly well, so BR decided to adopt a variation of GWR lined dark green (Middle Chrome green) for its passenger classes, with the result that the 'Kings' reverted to a colour scheme similar to that worn prior to Nationalisation.

In fact, ex-GWR locomotives experienced little change in outward appearance as a result of Nationalisation. Whereas the locomotives of the other former companies were renumbered, those of the GWR retained their old numbers because these were cast as metal plates (made of brass in

Above: No. 6000 King George V is seen here in blue livery, which it retained until April 1952. The former semi-streamliner, No. 6014, was the last blue 'King', at least until 6023 King Edward II was launched in 2011. (Roy Vandersteen collection)

Right: In traditional lined green livery, No. 6015 King Edward III backs into Paddington station on 18 August 1962 as a pannier tank removes a train of empty stock. (Geoff Rixon)

(any cases) affixed to their cab sides.

However, the transfer numbers on the bufferbeams were replaced by cast iron number plates fixed to brackets welded on the smokebox door, which was extremely unhelpful in the case of express locomotives such as the 'Kings' (except former semi-streamliner No. 6014). This was because the large train reporting numbers usually carried by these engines when working trains concealed the front numberplate. With the bufferbeam number now discontinued, the locomotives often became unidentifiable in photographs. On the other hand, it must be said that bufferbeam numbers were not always legible either, because of the angle of viewpoint or because the bufferbeam was too dirty.

Left and below: No identification problems here despite the train reporting numbers. No. 6021 King Richard II enters Exeter St David's on 18 July 1953 with the 10am train from Newquay to Paddington and resplendent No. 6029 King Edward VIII approaches the sea wall near Dawlish after passing through Teignmouth station on 19 July 1953 with a Plymouth–Paddington train.
(Geoff Rixon)

Other post-war modifications

Following No. 6022's improved performance, resulting from the fitting of the four-row superheated boiler, the entire 'King' class received this modification between 1949 and 1951. In addition, the whole class was fitted with mechanical lubricators, also pioneered on No. 6022. With high-superheat engines, it was all the more important to ensure the right amount of oil was fed to the cylinders and valves, and these lubricators were pre-set, thereby avoiding the possible 'hit-or-miss' manual lubrication carried out by drivers. The oil supply was determined by the position of the regulator while the lubricating pipes from the boiler to the smokebox were covered by a flat box located near the top of the boiler/smokebox on the driver's side (the right-hand side looking forwards) of the locomotive. The lubricators were on the same side, initially mounted on the running plate behind the outside steam pipe, but for ease of access to the inside

motion, were later moved to a position immediately in front of the steam pipe.

Around the same time, a squared steel plate was fitted to the edge of the inside valve cover on all the 'Kings', to provide additional grip for personnel working around the front of the smokebox. This replaced the original curved edging.

Indifferent coal and less-frequent servicing continued to be a problem for the Western Region's express passenger locomotives in the early 1950s, and experiments were undertaken to increase steaming capacity and decrease the amount of servicing required at depots. Self-cleaning arrangements in the smokebox, whereby the ashes from the fire were broken down and exited the locomotive through the chimney instead of having to be shovelled out manually from the bottom of the smokebox, were introduced. This reduced manual labour and meant installing baffles and mesh plates in the smokebox.

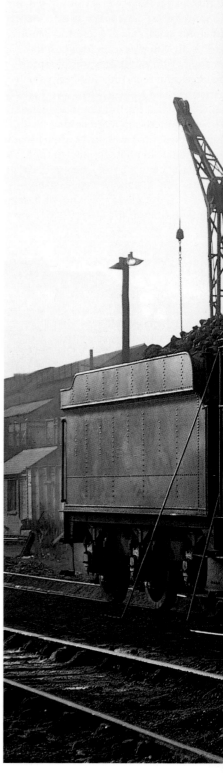

These factors resulted in initial alterations to the blastpipe and chimney design. The consequent improved draughting enabled the engines to steam more freely and cope better with inferior coal, as well as counteracting the detrimental effect on steaming which would otherwise have arisen from the self-cleaning smokebox equipment. Nos 6001 and 6017 were the first of the class to receive these modifications, in the autumn of 1952, and which were subsequently extended to the remainder of the class. Modified engines were fitted with a small metal plate fixed immediately below the shed code plate on the smokebox door, bearing the initials 'SC' (for self-cleaning, not, as some thought, for 'shed code'!).

The fitting of new boilers to the 'King' class with higher superheating and improved draughting design brought about an immediate improvement in steaming, offering the possibility of accelerating services and at least, restoring pre-war timings regardless of the quality of the coal. With this objective in mind, more extensive trials were undertaken with No. 6001 *King Edward VII*, both on the stationary plant at Swindon Works in the spring of 1953 and on special test trains in the subsequent July, running between Reading and Stoke Gifford (where Bristol Parkway station is now located). These trains comprised up to 25 coaches weighing almost 800 tons and, being fitted in between normal services, were required

to maintain normal speeds for express passenger trains. No. 6001's performance with this heavy load was outstanding, the 73½ miles being covered in just under 77 minutes, with speeds in the region of 80mph reached.

These tests, which involved the use of hard and soft coal, proved that, as a result of the modifications, No. 6001 could achieve a steaming rate of 25,000lb/hr, an increase of some 30 per cent over the steaming capacity of 'Kings' without improved draughting. Furthermore, modified 'Kings' would now have enough in reserve to maintain the proposed faster schedules when working trains of normal weight, even when provided with inferior coal.

Below: Three years after its draughting trials, and following the fitting of a double chimney, No. 6001 King Edward VII approaches the Arrivals side of Paddington station. (Alan Sainty collection)

Post-war accelerated services

The 'Bristolian'

From the summer of 1954, with track improvements having been carried out across the Western Region, express passenger services were to be accelerated between London and Bristol. The most important train was the non-stop 'Bristolian' express whose name had been revived in 1951.

The 'Bristolian' was now to cover the journey between Paddington and Bristol Temple Meads once again in 1¾hr (105min), as in pre-war days. (Prior to the accelerated schedule it was taking 140min.) Building in recovery time of 8min for permanent way slacks, etc., running time would be limited to 97min, requiring an average speed of 73mph to be maintained. However, the load would be light – a mere seven coaches weighing approximately 250 tons loaded.

A test run was arranged on 30 April 1954 using a 'King' with improved draughting (No. 6003 *King George IV*), hauling seven coaches and a dynamometer car, the train weighing 260 tons gross. The special started from Paddington and travelled down via Bath, was routed

around Bristol, rather than entering Temple Meads, and returned via Badminton. (The actual routing of the 'Bristolian' was travelling down to Bristol Temple Meads via Bath, returning via Badminton.) Apart from two brief stops outside Bristol (at Dr Day's Bridge Junction and Stapleton Road), and an unavoidable crawl between these two points, this was intended to be a continuous high speed run from Paddington to Bristol and back. This objective was certainly achieved.

Despite a permanent way slack of 18mph at Shrivenham, the 117.9 miles from Paddington to Dr Day's Bridge Junction was covered in 99.25min, with a maximum speed of 96.5mph being achieved down Dauntsey Bank. On the return journey, the 116 miles from Stapleton Road to Paddington was covered in 95.5min, with

Above: The pre-accelerated 'Bristolian' headed by No. 6013 King Henry VIII prepares to depart from Paddington on 3 July 1952. (A.R. Carpenter/ Transport Treasury)

Left: The locomotive used on the high speed 'Bristolian' special, No. 6003 King George IV, is seen some three years later, on 28 May 1957, at Knowle & Dorridge hauling the 2.35pm from Birkenhead to Paddington. (Michael Mensing)

Above: With twice as many carriages in tow than on a weekday, this non-accelerated Saturday working of the down 'Bristolian' was photographed near Hayes & Harlington on 10 July 1954 with No. 6002 King William IV at its head. (A. Lathey/Transport Treasury)

a top speed of 93mph being reached at Little Somerford. Excluding the time and distance between Dr Day's Bridge Junction and Stapleton Road, the remaining 233.9 miles were covered in 194.75min, making the average speed a creditable 72.3mph. The special arrived at both Bristol and Paddington with several minutes in hand.

The stage was now set for the first post-war accelerated running of the 'Bristolian', which took place on 14 June 1954, the start of the Summer timetable, with the flagship locomotive, No. 6000 *King George V*, naturally doing the honours. This run makes an interesting comparison with the inaugural run by No. 6000 19 years earlier, on 31 August 1935, when time was lost on the return journey, resulting in a mad dash over the last few miles, with Old Oak Common passed at 88mph and arrival at Paddington only 0.5min late. On this 1954 inaugural run, with the benefit of the 'King's' improved draughting,

speed was far more even, confirming that the class was capable of sustained high speed running when required. Even with a permanent way slack which caused the train to be four minutes late passing Wootton Bassett, No. 6000 arrived at Paddington nearly three minutes early. The inaugural down journey with No. 6000 had also been impressive, with Bristol Temple Meads being reached 3½ minutes early.

With its booked average speed of 67.6mph on the down train via Bath, and 67.2mph on the return working via Badminton, this was now the fastest advertised steam working in the world. However, although 'Kings' had initially been rostered to haul the post-war 'Bristolian', mainly for prestige reasons, it was found that 'Castles' with improved draughting were also capable of maintaining the train's 105min schedule as it was so lightly loaded. Indeed, on 17 April 2010, Tyseley's 'Castle' No. 5043 *Earl*

of Mount Edgcumbe replicated the 'Bristolian' working, but with a train weighing an extra 50 tons (due to the addition of a water carrier), and completed the up journey in an astounding 110min, with an average speed of 64.2mph despite being limited to an official maximum of 75mph!

Another advantage of using 'Castles' on the 'Bristolian' was that they provided greater flexibility as regards rostering because, when 'Kings' were used, the same engine that worked the down train also worked the up train, resulting in the 'King' lying idle at Bristol between 10.30am and 4.30pm. However, 'Kings' continued to be employed on the 'Bristolian' when the loadings were heavier, notably on Fridays and, from 1957, also on Mondays.

Returning to 1954, further impressive performances on the 'Bristolian' by 'Kings' continued to occur and logs have been published of several of the initial workings. On Wednesday, 16 June, the third day of the accelerated 'Bristolian' service, No. 6015 *King Richard III* (not yet fitted with double blast pipe and double chimney) was in charge of the up train and, with some VIPs aboard, produced some fine running. The average speed on the five-mile uphill stretch (with a 1-in-300 gradient) between Winterbourne and Chipping Sodbury, was 71mph, increasing to an average speed of 75mph from Chipping Sodbury to Badminton (another five-mile stretch with the same gradient). Badminton was passed in 18min 51sec from Temple Meads and the train swept through Swindon at close on 85mph. The east end of Goring and Streatley yard was cleared exactly one hour from leaving Temple Meads, a distance of 72.3 miles. The total journey time from Bristol to Paddington was 95min 1sec, i.e. arriving nearly ten minutes early.

On the previous day, 15 June, the 'Bristolian' had apparently arrived at Paddington six minutes early, whereas on the first day, 14 June, No. 6000 was barely three minutes early. No. 6015 was also in charge on 17 June and completed the up journey of 117.6 miles in 96min 12sec, arriving 8min 48sec early. On 1 July, No. 6000, hauling 280 tons gross (due to the inclusion of an extra carriage) brought the up 'Bristolian' into Paddington our minutes early, having averaged an impressive 70.2mph over the ten-mile scent from Winterborne to Badminton, nd reaching 91mph at Little Somerford. No. 6000 also worked the express on 21 uly and on the up journey averaged more han 81mph for the 98.7 miles between adminton and Westbourne Park, reaching Paddington an amazing 8min 41sec early.

No. 6015 *King Richard III* was clearly a star performer and was frequently used on the 'Bristolian', particularly in these early weeks. Hauling the down train on both 22 and 23 June, it was early reaching Temple Meads by 4min 43sec and 3min 27sec respectively, with top speeds of 90mph and 91mph respectively at Dauntsey. No. 6015's up working on 22 June was also notable, bringing the train into

Paddington 7min 55sec early.

An even more spectacular performance occurred when No. 6018 *King Henry VI* hauled a down working during these early months of the accelerated 'Bristolian' when the eminent train recorder O.S. Nock was on the footplate. (Unfortunately, the actual date does not seem to have been published.) There had been a succession of

Below: The star of the early fast runnings of the 'Bristolian' in 1954, No. 6015 King Richard III, exudes power as it waits to depart from Paddington station a few years later. (Author's collection)

the foot of the incline, achieving an average speed of 100mph between mileposts 87 and 89. This was the highest speed ever clocked personally by O.S. Nock for a steam locomotive on the Western Region and is believed to be the fastest authenticated speed attained by a single-chimney 'King'.

The timings quoted above are actual ones but, as mentioned earlier, the schedule allowed for permanent way slacks, signal stops, etc., resulting in net timings. The fastest known net time achieved by steam on the 'Bristolian' was in 1958 when No. 6015 *King Richard III*, hauling 300 tons gross and by now fitted with a double blastpipe and chimney, completed the down journey in 92min net (109min 24sec actual time as a result of severe speed restrictions and signal stops). The train would have arrived at Bristol considerably later had there not been some extremely fast bursts of speed such as a frightening 88mph through Reading, 89mph at Cholsey, and 98mph down Dauntsey Bank. On another occasion around the same period, No. 6019 *King Henry V* hauled a down working of the 'Bristolian' with three extra

coaches added, for which an allowance of five minutes had been added to the schedule. The train covered the 77.3 miles between Paddington and Swindon in an amazing 62min and is believed to have arrived at Bristol five minutes early against the normal schedule (10min early taking account of the extra allowance).

The 'Bristolian' ceased to be Britain's fastest train in the summer of 1958, its 67.6mph average speed being overtaken by the Eastern Region's 67.8mph average attained between Darlington and York on a Newcastle to King's Cross service. In an effort to regain its record, the Western Region considered reducing the 'Bristolian' schedule to 100min and carried out a test run on 22 May 1958 with No. 6018 *King Henry VI*. There was also a trial run some two weeks earlier with a 'Castle', but abandoned the proposal in the light of permanent way slacks encountered. However, a little over a year later, the 'Bristolian' was able to be scheduled for 100min when diesel-hydraulics replaced steam from 15 June 1959, thus ending 'King' and 'Castle' scheduled operation on this prestigious service.

Above: As it approaches Slough station on 12 July 1959, No. 6018 King Henry VI is certainly travelling, albeit not at 102.5mph, but fast enough, had it been on the up relief line, to rattle the stuffed dog's glass cabinet on the platform (still there today)! (Geoff Rixon)

Right: Just days before steam was replaced by diesel, No. 6019 King Henry V waits at Paddington with the down 'Bristolian' on 11 June 1959. (Alan Sainty collection)

Opposite: This iconic view against the backdrop of Horse Shoe Cove, west of Dawlish in Devon, epitomises the GWR's marketing image of being the Holiday Line, and features the down 'Cornish Riviera Express' hauled by No. 6009 King Charles II around 1934. (Railway Wonders of the World)

slight checks before Swindon, although the train was still two minutes ahead of schedule at this point. Nevertheless, the crew decided to 'have a go', passing the crest of Dauntsey Bank at 88mph and reaching 102.5mph at

The 'Cornish Riviera Express'

The 'Kings' were employed on several titled trains during their lifetime, but the one most closely associated with the class, which they monopolised for over 30 years and which is referred to several times in this book in order to demonstrate the capabilities of the class, was the 'Cornish Riviera Express'.

When the 'King' class took over the 'Cornish Riviera' in 1927 from the 'Castle' class, which were becoming insufficiently powerful for the increasingly heavily loaded service, the scheduled journey time for the non-stop run from Paddington to Plymouth was reduced by ten minutes to a straight four hours. This required the 173.5 miles between Paddington and Exeter to be travelled in 168min. In addition, the load limit for unpiloted trains over the Devon banks was increased to 360 tons. On arrival at Plymouth, a lighter locomotive had to haul the train for the remainder of the journey to Penzance because, during their working lives, 'Kings' were too heavy to travel across Brunel's Royal Albert Bridge at Saltash. They have been able to since, in preservation, because the bridge has been strengthened.

'Kings' are, however, alleged to have made occasional forays across the bridge on passenger trains before it was strengthened, although any such occurrences do not seem to have been authenticated by photographic proof, and therefore remain doubtful. The furthest west that 'Kings' were normally allowed to venture was Keyham, just east of Westonmill Viaduct and the Royal Albert Bridge. On Sundays the Travelling Post Office train, normally a 'Castle' working but sometimes hauled by a 'King', terminated at Plymouth North Road, the train engine then placing the empty stock in a siding at Keyham for stabling during the day.

Twenty-five years after the service had commenced, new 60ft carriages for the 'Cornish Riviera' were introduced. The inaugural running of this stock took place on 8 July 1929, the train hauled by No. 6000 *King George V*, it being despatched from Paddington by Collett himself, ringing the engine's American bell (it must still have had its clapper then!). The new stock,

however, was destined to form part of the 'Cornish Riviera' for a mere six years because, in 1935, in recognition of 100 years having passed since its inception, the GWR introduced even newer, wide-bodied carriages on the express, called not surprisingly, Centenary stock.

Also in 1935, the 'Cornish Riviera' started to be run in two portions, the first one being advertised as non-stop to Truro, taking 5hr 25min to cover the distance of 279.25 miles from Paddington. The train would normally consist of 14 carriages weighing some 500 tons full.

Upon the outbreak of the Second World War in September 1939, the 'Cornish Riviera' became affected by new restrictions put in place, including a speed limit of 60mph (albeit raised to 75mph in 1941). Following the end of the war, the GWR accelerated the service in an attempt to reach pre-war timings, but the extremely severe winter of 1946/7 caused havoc,

particularly in respect of coal supplies, and forced the temporary withdrawal of the service. When the train resumed operation for the summer of 1947, it was still slower than pre-war standards and, by this time, it was becoming heavier again.

The normal load on summer Saturdays was 14 or 15 coaches, mainly through the attraction of the West Country and, in particular, Cornwall, with its 'Riviera' regarded as a holiday paradise (the lure of the Mediterranean was yet to come). Another factor was the continuing reliance on the railways for travel in Britain because, even after the end of petrol rationing, private car ownership was still not yet widespread.

For 1955, the intention was to revert to the four-hour Paddington–Plymouth schedule and by this time, the modifications being made to the 'King' class, which greatly improved their performance, made this objective possible. Nevertheless, there were critics who doubted the might of the

Above: With a light load of only 12 coaches, No. 6025 King Henry III brings the up 'Cornish Riviera' along the sea wall at Dawlish on a desolate day in 1954. (Jim Jarvis)

Left: You can almost feel the cold in this picture of No. 6029 King Edward VIII hauling the down 'Cornish Riviera' past admiring holidaymakers between Dawlish and Teignmouth in July (yes!) 1953. (Geoff Rixon)

'Kings', arguing that a Pacific locomotive would produce a better performance. Consequently, between March and May 1955, dynamometer car tests were run on the 'Cornish Riviera Express' between an unprepared 'King', No. 6013 *King Henry VIII*, and 'Princess Coronation' ('Duchess') class No. 46237 *City of Bristol*.

The trials are covered in more detail in the section Final Steaming Improvements, but suffice to say at this point, that a Pacific was found to perform no better than a 'King' on these trains. The result of this was the four-hour schedule reintroduced in Summer 1955, with 'Kings' in charge.

In the post-war period, there were sometimes variations in the way the 'Cornish Riviera' was operated, for example, removing the 'King' at Newton Abbot (the locomotive then double

heading a subsequent train in order to reach Plymouth), with the first passenger stop being at Truro, and the main part of the train going to St Ives, with only a few coaches going to Penzance. Also, in the height of the holiday season the 'Cornish Riviera' was often divided into several different portions, running as separate trains. For a time, the 'King' was taken off at Devonport on summer Saturdays. The class continued to hold sway on the 'Limited' as it had since 1927, except on rare occasions such as engineering works if the train was diverted on to lines over which the 'Kings' were banned. In 1958, their reign ended when diesel-hydraulics took over haulage of this service and by the 1960s the halcyon days of the 'Cornish Riviera Express' had passed as increasing numbers of holidaymakers

travelled to the West Country by their own private car. It is a remarkable achievement that the 'Kings' worked this prestigious and very demanding service for more than 30 years.

The 'Cornish Riviera Express' was the GWR's and BR Western Region's crack express, its equivalent to, say, the 'Golden Arrow', 'Royal Scot' and 'Flying Scotsman' of the other railways/regions. Competition had been rife between the GWR and the Southern Railway for the lucrative West Country passenger traffic but, until the arrival of the 'Merchant Navy' Pacifics in 1941, the SR had no locomotives comparable with the 'Kings' in terms of power. Nor did the Southern have the same opportunities as the GWR for high speed running by avoiding unwanted stops because it did not use slip coaches or water troughs.

Above: In this June 1959 view, the tender scoop on No. 6019 King Henry V collects water from the troughs at Goring, between Reading and Didcot. Pity the passengers in the first carriage if the windows are open because they will be receiving a cold shower, as will the photographer if he is not wearing waterproofs! (Geoff Rixon)

Left: With its mechanical lubricator in the initial position behind the outside steam pipe, No. 6025 King Henry III brings the down 'Cornish Riviera' into Exeter St David's in July 1953. (Geoff Rixon)

The Birmingham line

Acceleration was also a priority on the London–Birmingham line. As with the West Country expresses, stops had been avoided by using slip coaches, although by the time of the outbreak of the Second World War, average speed timings had deteriorated as there were fewer two-hour trains, and by the early post-war years the best time was 2.25hr with the average being closer to 2.5hr. However, two-hour timings, albeit only one train in each direction each day, titled the 'Inter City', were restored in 1953.

Remaining trains still took 2.5hr, although in the following year the 'Cambrian Coast Express' was reintroduced and became another two-hour express between Paddington and Birmingham. Several factors inhibited the running of more trains on the faster timings, notably track occupation difficulties arising from the increased volume of freight traffic, and the numerous local trains in the London and Birmingham areas. Also, there were heavy loadings due to trains continuing beyond Birmingham to Wolverhampton and Shrewsbury.

Left and opposite: No. 6001 King Edward VII speeds through Knowle & Dorridge with the 8.5am Birkenhead–Paddington express on 4 August 1957, and No. 6025 King Henry III breasts the summit at The Hawthorns halt near West Bromwich, with the down 'Cambrian Coast Express' on 16 September 1961. (Michael Mensing)

Below: After leaving Snow Hill Tunnel, No. 6012 King Edward VI accelerates past something 'unmentionable' at Birmingham Moor Street as it makes its way to London with the 'Inter-City' on 7 September 1961. (Michael Mensing)

Right: On 16 February 1956, welcome intruder No. 46254 City of Stoke-on-Trent leaves Paddington's Platform 1 with the 11.15am 'Merchant Venturer'. (Colin Hogg)

Below: Just over a year before it nearly lost a wheel, No. 6018 King Henry VI thunders along the up relief line at Purley-on-Thames, between Pangbourne and Tilehurst, and into the camera lens of one of the PW gang, as it heads the 1.37pm Bristol–Paddington express on 6 March 1955. (Ian Nash)

Trouble down below

Amid the euphoria over the improved draughting, creating opportunities for high speed running, not everything was going well for the 'Kings' – they were in fact cracking up, literally. More than 25 years' of strenuous work hauling the heaviest trains was beginning to take its toll. In the latter part of January 1956, major cracks were discovered in the bogies which were too significant to be repaired by simple welding, as had been carried out over the previous years when minor cracks were discovered. More substantial repairs were urgently required, involving the welding of strengthening bars on the bogie frames. Consequently, the class was withdrawn from service for a few days and two 'Coronations' ('Duchesses'), Nos 46254 *City of Stoke-on-Trent* and 46257 *City of Salford*, were drafted in from the London Midland Region to help take the heaviest trains, while 'Castles' deputised for much of the remainder of the 'Kings'' work.

No sooner had the bogie frames been repaired, cracks were noticed in the front section of the main frames. The class was again withdrawn, this time to enable part of their frames to be cut away and new front sections welded on. Two further LMR Pacifics were loaned by the London Midland Region, 'Princess Royal' class Nos 46207 *Princess Arthur of Connaught* and 46210 *Lady Patricia*. In addition, several BR Standard Class 5s (Nos 73xxx series) were borrowed, taking over some 'Castle' duties, thereby enabling the latter to take on heavier trains normally hauled by 'Kings'. The Pacifics all returned home in late February 1956.

Unfortunately, it was only a couple of months before another problem was found with the 'Kings' – fractured driving axles. In April 1956, a signalman at Waltham, near Maidenhead, who fortunately was more alert than those at Shrivenham in 1936, was watching No. 6018 *King Henry VI* go hurtling by on an express and noticed the centre driving wheel was wobbling. He

Above and page 79:
Two Birmingham line
'regulars' fitted with
Alfloc water treatment
equipment in the 1950s,
were No. 6005 King
George II, seen approaching
Lapworth after a signal
stop on 15 June 1958, and
No. 6009 King Charles II
leaving Birmingham Snow
Hill with the up Saturday
'Cambrian Coast Express'
on 4 July 1959. (Michael
Mensing)

immediately had the train stopped and, on examination, the axle was found to be broken in two, yet the wobbly driving wheels had been undetected on the footplate. Had the train continued on its journey, the locomotive could have lost a wheel and possibly derailed with catastrophic consequences. However, it must be said that when 'Saint' class 4-6-0 No. 2933 *Bilbury Court* suddenly became a 4-5-0 at Olton on 1 February 1930, when hauling a Birkenhead-bound express (axle breakage resulted in one of the front pair of driving wheels ending up in a ditch), the footplate crew, realising that something

was wrong, halted the train and the locomotive remained on the track.

Further work carried out around this time was the provision of new cylinders, along with new outside steam pipes to eliminate the frequent breakages that were occurring, and the front casing over the inside cylinders was altered. In addition, 17 members of the class were fitted with Alfloc water treatment equipment, these being the locomotives used on Birmingham line trains because of the quality of water in the West Midlands. This equipment led to improvements in steaming through a

reduction of scale forming on the heating surfaces, which also enabled the frequency of boiler washouts to be reduced.

Also, larger front buffers were fitted as the smaller GWR ones could become entangled with the new hydraulic buffer stops which were being introduced across the region. Bearing in mind that the whole class had also received new boilers, the Western Region authorities clearly considered the 'Kings', at this late stage in their lives, were worth the financial investment, and this was before the final modifications described below were carried out.

inal steaming improvements

mentioned in the section on the
ornish Riviera Express', Western Region
p management wanted this prestigious
ain to revert to a four-hour schedule
tween London and Plymouth from
e summer of 1955. This was a very
emanding requirement given the weight
the train – 14 coaches for the first 95
iles to Heywood Junction, where the
o Westbury slip coaches were detached
speed, and then 12 coaches onward to
ymouth. Furthermore, all 30 'Kings',
gardless of their condition, had to be
pable of taking this train and running
schedule; there was no question of this
eing a task exclusively for a select few
p performers.

However, there was some doubt about
hether the 'Kings', even with their
nproved draughting, were up to the job
nd so a further series of dynamometer car
sts was arranged, this time involving a
omparison between a 'King' (in this case,
very average and rather leaky example,
ot a hand-picked one), a London Midland
egion 'Princess Coronation' ('Duchess')
acific, and the unique 8P BR Standard
acific, No. 71000 *Duke of Gloucester*.
he trials took place between March
nd May 1955.

The performance of No. 71000 was
ainly determined by using the Swindon
ationary testing plant, although it did
ndertake some short road trials between
windon and Westbury. However, in the
ght of these tests, its power output was
und to be lower than that of a 'King'
nd so it was not tried on the 'Cornish
iviera Express'. The Southern and Eastern
egions did not participate and it became
two- horse contest between the 'Duchess',
o. 46237 *City of Bristol*, and the 'King',
o. 6013 *King Henry VIII*. The 'Duchess'
as tested on the London–Bristol and
ondon–Wolverhampton lines before
orking the 'Cornish Riviera' and, on its
rst attempt on 17 May, hauling the down
ain, put in an impressive performance,
ravelling the 193.6 miles to Newton Abbot
ell within the new, accelerated scheduled
me of 192min.

The 'King' had been tested first, when

weather conditions were not particularly
favourable, and it also performed
extremely well, achieving the fastest
recorded time between Paddington and
Exeter, on 10 March (159.25min, against
a scheduled time of 167.5min, for the
173.5 mile journey, and this despite two
permanent way slacks which cost 3.5min).
On the following day, hauling the up
'Cornish Riviera', the locomotive covered
the 173.5 miles in an astonishing
162min, but not without exhausting
the footplate crew.

Overall, there was little difference in
performance between the 'King' and the
Pacific, thus proving the point that the

4-6-0s could cope perfectly well with the
accelerated 'Cornish Riviera' timings,
despite the heavy loadings.

However, a weakness in the 'King's'
design following re-draughting did become
apparent in these trials. Both *City of Bristol*
and *Duke of Gloucester* were fitted with a
double blastpipe and double chimney and
this brought about an improvement in
draughting, enhancing overall efficiency
as well as reducing coal consumption. It is
perhaps surprising that Swindon was so
slow in recognising the benefits of double
blastpipes and chimneys. These features
had been pioneered in France in 1933
and the LNER, having noted the amazing

*Below: Some six years after
its remarkable performance
on test, No. 6013 King
Henry VIII is seen hard at
work between Olton and
Solihull hauling the 6.45am
Wolverhampton–Paddington
express on 6 July 1961.*
(Michael Mensing)

performance of the engines in question, wasted no time in fitting them to the P2 class 2-8-2 No. 2001 *Cock o' the North* and some of the A4s, including the record-beating locomotive, *Mallard*.

The LMS was also convinced and fitted double blastpipes and chimneys to the 'Princess Coronation' Pacifics and the rebuilt 'Royal Scots', an example of the latter type performing spectacularly on the Western Region during the 1948 Locomotive Exchanges. Yet it was not until 1955 that the Western Region decided to install these modifications in one of their engines, selecting No. 6015 *King Richard III* as the guinea pig. Early experiences with this engine were favourable and so it was rostered to haul the 'Cornish Riviera' on 26 September 1955, with some important officials on board. The engine's performance was outstanding, with speeds

in excess of 100mph being achieved on stretches where the top speed was normally around 85mph, with a maximum of 103mph being recorded at Lavington. In addition, there was a marked improvement in hill climbing ability, a considerable increase in the hourly rate of steam production, and a noticeable decrease in water and coal consumption.

With more officials on board, No. 6015 was rostered to haul the down 'Cornish Riviera' again, three days later and where 103mph had been attained on 26 September, this time 108.5mph was recorded. This was the highest authenticated speed ever achieved by a 'King', putting this class in third equal place with the LNER A3 class, behind the LMS 'Coronation' class (114mph) and of course, the LNER A4 class (126mph), all larger machines being 4-6-2s.

Further dynamometer car trials took place in May 1956, this time with another modified 'King', No. 6002 *King William IV*, on both the Birmingham line and the West of England main line. The locomotive's performance was outstanding, showing the engine's ability to recover lost time through signal stops and permanent way slacks, and still arrive ahead of schedule.

The trials also demonstrated beyond doubt, the superiority of the double-chimney 'Kings' over the single-chimney ones with improved draughting, enabling the modified ones to deliver all that was required of them in terms of operating the accelerated schedules with heavy loadings. Consequently, the decision was taken to convert all 30 'Kings', culminating in No. 6008 *King James II* in December 1958. The first 14 of the

Below: The pioneer that brought a new lease of life to the 'Kings', No. 6015 King Richard III, simmers at Newton Abbot in August 1959. (LRTA collection)

 class to be converted were fitted with somewhat inelegant straight-sided double chimneys, but these were quickly replaced by more attractive, elliptical-shaped chimneys which the remainder of the class also received.

In the 'King' class, the Western Region now had a fleet of virtually new locomotives. Unfortunately, this coincided with the arrival of the first diesel-hydraulics which were intended to replace them as quickly as possible. Ripe for another 20 years of top-link service, the 'Kings' were even due to receive new roller bearings for all axles, and an initial order for eight engines was fulfilled in 1957–8, but the bearings were never fitted. By the end of 1962 the whole class had been withdrawn – a shocking waste of money, particularly since Swindon was still overhauling 'Kings' earlier that year.

Above: No. 6002 King William IV has just been piloted over the Devon banks as it arrives at Plymouth North Road with the down 'Royal Duchy' on 19 September 1959. (Alan Sainty collection)

Left: Before modification, No. 6008 King James II shows off its beautiful single chimney one last time at Plymouth (Laira). Bring it on, No. 6023! (Roy Vincent/Transport Treasury)

Increased route availability

The final years of the 'Kings' in service showed them at the peak of their performance despite the fact they were around thirty years old by now. As stated previously, the 'Kings'' heavy axle loading, resulting in their 'double-red' restricted route availability, had confined them, in GWR days, to just a few lines: Paddington–Plymouth (including Millbay Docks, albeit not initially) via Bath/Badminton and Bristol; Paddington–Wolverhampton via Bicester, and Newton Abbot–Kingswear. They continued to operate these routes after Nationalisation in 1948 throughout most of the 1950s and into the 1960s.

In BR days, 'Kings' also ventured into some new territory. On 1 February 1949, No. 6000 *King George V* hauled the first official 'King'-hauled passenger train through Severn Tunnel. 'Kings' had in fact passed through Severn Tunnel before but this was either unofficially or on test. From 5 to 16 February 1938, Nos 6004 *King George III* and 6015 *King Richard III* were based at Bristol in order to undertake clearance tests on Sundays through the tunnel and onwards to Newport and Ebbw Vale.

For these tests the locomotives hauled extremely heavy coal trains. Apparently, these trains, weighing up to 1,350 tons, had a 'King' at each end and it has been suggested the main purpose of the tests was to evaluate a proposal to construct a class of two-cylinder 2-10-2 tank engines fitted with 'King' boilers, which seems an extraordinary proposition, if it is true. In any event, the GWR made do with its 2-8-0 and 2-8-2 tanks for this traffic and no further haulage of coal trains by 'Kings' seems to have occurred. Neither were there any scheduled workings by 'Kings' through Severn Tunnel until No. 6000's inaugural passenger trip in 1949. This led to the use of 'Kings' to haul passenger trains on

Right: Far from its home at Old Oak Common in June 1959, No. 6019 King Henry V stands at Plymouth North Road station, the official extent of 'King' operation westwards during their BR operational life.
(Geoff Rixon)

Right: One of two choices trialled on coal trains, No. 6004 King George III is pictured on normal duties as it stands at the western end of Bristol Temple Meads station with the 4.15pm Paddington–Plymouth on 9 May 1958. Beyond is Bristol (Bath Road) engine shed, enticing yet frustratingly distant for spotters on the platform.
(Michael Mensing)

he North & West route from Newport to hrewsbury via Severn Tunnel in 1951. Iowever, they had previously ventured hrough the tunnel working newspaper nd parcel trains, this being a Bristol Bath oad duty for the handful allocated there.

In 1953, the reconstruction of Shifnal iaduct between Wolverhampton and hrewsbury enabled 'Kings' to cross this tructure, although, as a result of some latform clearance problems, the class was

not regularly used on this route until 1959.

With the introduction of diesel hydraulics on the West of England main line in 1958, and on London to Bristol services in the following year, the use of 'Kings' on these routes was severely reduced, albeit not entirely eliminated. Nevertheless, the regular use of 'Kings' in late 1959 on the South Wales main line from Paddington to Cardiff provided some alternative work for the class. Sporadic use

had started in 1955 following clearance and bridge tests back in 1952 when plans to use them on the 'Red Dragon' titled train were first proposed, but then abandoned at that time. Passenger services between London and South Wales during the 1950s were often in the hands of BR Standards ('Britannia' Pacifics), but these were relegated to less-important duties when the 'Kings' took over in force. The 'Kings'' Indian summer on South Wales

Above: Having taken over from a 'Hall' class locomotive, which has brought the train to Cardiff (General) over lines prohibited to 'Kings', No. 6003 King George IV sets off for London with the 'Red Dragon', in September 1960. (Alan Jarvis)

expresses, when six of the class were allocated to Cardiff (Canton), lasted until March 1962 when 'Hymek' diesels were introduced on these services.

On all the aforementioned routes, the 'Kings' by no means held the monopoly prior to the introduction of diesels. Many of the workings were well within the capabilities of the 'Castle' class, particularly since some of these locomotives had, like the 'Kings', been fitted with double blast pipes and double chimneys. This was particularly the case with the North & West route and London–Bristol services. Nevertheless, the 'Kings' were there to haul the heaviest trains and they performed their duties with honour.

All references in this book to 'Kings' at work are about their usage on passenger duties, mainly of a prestigious nature. Nevertheless, they did appear from time to time on non-passenger trains. For the purpose of running-in following overhaul, 'Kings' would normally be used on local passenger trains in the Swindon area, but they could also be seen working the Sunday afternoon van train from Paddington to Swindon.

The milk trains from the West Country and West Wales to London were regarded as lucrative traffic by the GWR and the Western Region of BR, and therefore not beneath the dignity of the 'King' class, although 'Castles' were more frequently used.

Far left: By now permitted to venture north west beyond Wolverhampton, No. 6018 King Henry VI stands at Shrewsbury in June 1961. (Alan Sainty collection)

Left: Viewed from 'Jacob's Ladder' at West Ealing on 26 March 1961, No. 6027 King Richard I hurries along the down main line with a Sunday afternoon van train, believed to be a running-in turn. (Mike Pope)

Below: All dolled up to bring back the milk empties, No. 6012 King Edward VI has two trains in tow, probably assembled at West Ealing milk sidings from separate trains of previously filled wagons to other London destinations, such as White City. This train is approaching Southall station on the down relief line, although sometimes the empties train came down the main line. (Mike Pope)

Footplate experiences in BR days

Before moving on to the final BR workings and the subsequent preservation era, it seems appropriate to place on record some footplate experiences of a well-known BR fireman, R.S. (Dick) Potts, whose memories of firing and driving No. 6018 *King Henry VI* on the 'Farewell King' trip is described later. Dick Potts lives in retirement within a stone's throw of Tyseley Locomotive Works and Depot, and fired on 23 different 'Kings' between 1960 and 1962.

At the end of some of his trips as fireman, not just those made on 'Kings', Dick had the foresight to write up his experiences in case anyone should find these of interest in years to come. His notes and observations, covering journeys between Birmingham and Paddington, give a unique insight into life on the footplate of the Western Region's ultimate express locomotives in their final years, and are summarised as follows:

First trip: Wednesday, 25 May 1960
No. 6000 *King George V*
4.35pm Wolverhampton–Paddington
(The 'Inter City')
Boarded footplate at
Birmingham Snow Hill
12 coaches (407 tons)
Driver: J. Smith

Engine in good condition except for superheaters blowing badly. Highest speed 88mph just past Bicester. Unable to maintain full steam pressure on long stretches. 70mph through Banbury. Coal was good quality, soft, very dry with a lot of dust and very large lumps. Fire was quite clean on arrival at Paddington. Firing was continuous from Snow Hill to Saunderton, then very light and fire run down from Denham. Flap raised between each shovelful but firing not heavy for load nor was coal consumption for journey unduly heavy. Had departed Snow Hill 1min late. 30mph p/w check at Acocks Green. Arrived High Wycombe 8min early, departed on time. 60mph p/w check between Denham and Ruislip. Signal checks at Northolt East and West. 3min stop at Portobello signals. Arrived at Paddington 3min late.

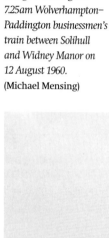

Below: A worm's eye view of No. 6000 King George V hauling the 7.25am Wolverhampton–Paddington businessmen's train between Solihull and Widney Manor on 12 August 1960. (Michael Mensing)

Second trip: Tuesday, 17 January 1961
No. 6020 *King Henry IV*
6.10pm Paddington–Birkenhead
(as far as Birmingham Snow Hill)
12 coaches (410 tons)
Driver: C. Taylor

Tender coaled with large eggs. Fire very low. Several shovelfuls put on mainly to the front before starting away. Water in boiler black caused by Alfloc chemicals. Slipped badly starting away from Paddington and Portobello Junction. After signal stop at

Ruislip unable to keep fire up, injector would not maintain water level. Front end lost in steam. Dust in eggs like sugar, water sprayed on had no effect. After signal check at Bicester, unable to feed front end properly due to large amount of egg dust which, when wet, would not leave the shovel. Coal well back down tender and had to be pulled down between firing which was almost continuous. Riding lively, inclined to bounce. Quiet except for seats which rattled badly.

Had departed Paddington on time. Signal stops at Westbourne Bridge, Ruislip (followed by 5–15mph restrictions), severe signal checks at Gerrards Cross and Beaconsfield due to Marylebone local train being in front, slight signal check at Tyler's Green, passed High Wycombe 12min late, 15mph p/w check at Bicester, signal stop at Aynho Junction, passed Banbury 19min late, 15mph p/w check at Fenny Compton, 22min late leaving Leamington. Arrived at Snow Hill 17min late.

Above: Consistent with Dick Potts's experience earlier in the year, No. 6020 King Henry IV does not appear to be in the best of condition as it steams (in every sense) through Haddenham with an up express from Birmingham in September 1960.
(John Beckett)

Third trip: Monday, 13 March 1961

No. 6020 *King Henry IV*
7.10pm Paddington–Wolverhampton
(as far as Birmingham Snow Hill)
10 coaches (348 tons)
Driver: F. Salmon

Coal stacked well in tender, mostly dusty stock coal with clinker and grass mixed in. Good fire in firebox but unable to lift back end with bar. Large smokeplate in place inclined to dip, doors shut a little to prevent this. Water level difficult to judge on journey as opening regulator filled glass. Water consumption heavy and right-hand injector unable to maintain boiler level if regulator on second valve. Clouds of steam from front end and bad continuous blow on driver's side, probably a steam pipe joint. Steaming well considering steam blows and quality of coal. Firing erratic to High Wycombe due to repeated signal checks but from then on more or less continuous to approach to Bicester.

Unable to fire fast due to lively riding of engine, so had to be steady but continuous.

Three shovels to front, then next six down the middle, but on several occasions had to fire to the bright patches due to fire losing its shape with large amount of dust. Usually, lumps put to the front and the dust to the back end. After the check at Claydon the flap chain came apart due to temporary repair by wire giving way and from then on the doors were used and closed up to within 1 inch. Riding very quiet, no vibration at all, no rattles or knocks, motion very tight but springs had too much give and also excessive amount of side play in axleboxes. Riding extremely lively at speed. Had departed Paddington on time. Signal checks at Old Oak West, Gerrards Cross, Beaconsfield, Tyler's Green, 2min late passing High Wycombe and also Ashendon, arrived and departed Bicester on time, signal check Banbury South, departed Banbury 1min late, 15mph slack at Claydon Crossing, 30mph slack at Fenny Compton, departed Leamington 7min late, departed Knowle 13min late, 15mph slack at Tyseley South. Arrived Snow Hill 6min late.

Below: Despite its suspect mechanical condition, No. 6020 King Henry IV is still going strong (well, at least still going!) on 11 June 1962, when photographed at Wolverhampton Low Level.

(Michael Mensing)

Fourth trip: Wednesday, 5 July 1961
No. 6011 *King James I*
6.10pm Paddington–Wolverhampton
(as far as Birmingham Snow Hill)
12 coaches (409 tons)
Driver: J. Payne

Extremely dirty. Cab filthy, footplate untidy. Soft coal, lot of lumps in the 'hole' but large amount of dust, very dry otherwise. Fire level with ring but made up with the shovel and unable to lift with the bar, nearly out at the front end.

Pressure dropped although numerous shovelfuls put to the front end and at Old Oak down to 180lb. Firing heavy to obtain correct shape. Flap up between each shovelful. From High Wycombe to Aynho pressure fixed at 240lb and at times flap not used between shovelling which was continuous and steady, but not heavy. Exhaust loud and clear especially between Bicester and Ardley. 72mph passing Bicester and only dropped to 66mph passing Ardley. No steam from front end.

Water taken at Aynho. Pressure 240lb at Hatton, large amount of dust baking fire, doors shut up to cut fire as middle of the grate not burning. Riding excellent, no vibration from motion and quiet running. Coal and water consumption very light. Had departed Paddington on time, severe signal check at Old Oak East and West, 2min late passing High Wycombe, stop at Saunderton due to signal failure, 4min late passing Banbury and leaving Leamington. Signal check at Bordesley North, arrived at Snow Hill on time.

Above: In contrast with Dick Potts's report, No. 6011 King James I looks fairly respectable as it hauls the 8.50am Birkenhead–Paddington express near Acock's Green on 25 September 1961. (Michael Mensing)

Above: Looking very smart on 15 April 1961, No. 6020 King Henry IV has just been coaled up in this view at Old Oak Common, which epitomises the dirty state of depots towards the end of steam. (Jim Oatway)

Fifth trip: Wednesday, 30 August 1961
No. 6020 *King Henry IV*
7.10pm Paddington–Wolverhampton
(as far as Birmingham Snow Hill)
10 coaches (341 tons)
Driver: H. Mason

Externally dirty. Large eggs. Bar in and pricker to push fire to front as fire out. Several shovelfuls to front before leaving. Firing light and almost confined to middle of the box. Dust kept down fairly well. 85mph near Brill and also at Fosse Road. Driver pulled coal forward at all stops and also did firing from Leamington. Flap not used from Gerrards Cross until Hatton Bank which was climbed at 50mph. Passed Olton at 75mph. Riding quiet and smooth. Footplate very clean at Paddington and front oiled down. No steam from front end, beats even and clear.

Had departed Paddington on time, 30mph slack at Old Oak East. Passed High Wycombe and Princes Risborough 2min early. Severe signal check at Haddenham. 2min late passing Ashendon Junction, 2min early arriving at Bicester. Severe signal check at Banbury South; arrived Banbury 3min late. 15mph slack at Banbury Junction, 4min late leaving Leamington, 40mph slack at Rowington, 7min late leaving Knowle; arrived Snow Hill on time.

Sixth trip: Friday, 1 September 1961

No. 6014 *King Henry VII*
7.10pm Paddington–Wolverhampton
(as far as Birmingham Snow Hill)
10 coaches (341 tons)
Driver: H. Neal

Externally fairly clean. Footplate tidy but dirty. Wedge cab. Soft coal, only small lumps. Good fire, bar put in back before leaving Paddington. Steaming well, firing heavy to Gerrards Cross. Lever rack rattled slightly and beat slightly uneven but very strong and free running. Side rods knocked slightly but no vibration felt in cab. Riding quiet and springy, some violent tail wagging at times. Steaming much better when firing small coal and dust, and at back end. Firing confined to centre of grate, fire level just above ring. Coal consumption reasonable, water consumption a bit above normal. Flap used between shovelfuls to Beaconsfield, but between every six from then on. Doors opened frequently to prevent blowing off. 80mph at Brill and Fosse Road, 75mph at Haddenham, Ayhno Park and Olton, passed Hatton in eight minutes with doors open. When on second valve, continuous stream of sparks up chimney. No steam from front end, slight blow from pressure valves at times.

Had departed Paddington on time, 20mph slack at Old Oak East, passed High Wycombe and Princes Risborough 2min early, arrived Bicester 4min early, left 1min late. 15mph slack at Banbury Junction, 60mph restriction at Fenny Compton. Arrived and departed Leamington 4min late, Hatton passed 2min late, signal check Hatton North, 40mph restriction at Rowington, arrived and departed Knowle 4min late, arrived Snow Hill 3min early.

Below: Recognisable by its wedge-shaped cab, former semi-streamliner No. 6014 King Henry VII approaches Solihull with the 11.45 Birkenhead to Paddington express on Easter Sunday, 17 April 1960. (Michael Mensing)

Seventh trip: Wednesday, 6 June 1962
No. 6000 *King George V*
5pm Birmingham–Paddington
(The 'Inter City')
10 coaches (350 tons)
Driver: J.R. Davies

Externally very clean. Handed over by Stafford Road crew in excellent condition. Good fire, clean. Good soft coal. Firing very light, doors open for about half the journey, no difficulty in maintaining pressure above 225lb. Riding excellent and quiet, except for slight knock on lever rack. Side rods knocking slightly. Very free running. Touched 90mph near Brill and 80mph at Greenford (after Denham check). Scoop stuck at Rowington, very hard to operate and float unreliable. Had departed Snow Hill on time, Leamington and Banbury still on time, then severe check, 3min late passing Ardley; arrived High Wycombe 4min early. Departed High Wycombe 1min late, stopped at Denham and told to pass failed signal at West Ruislip, arrived Paddington 1min late.

Eighth trip: Wednesday, 6 June 1962
No. 6017 *King Edward IV*
8.10pm Paddington–Birmingham
12 coaches (415 tons)
Driver: J.R. Davies

Externally very dirty. Handed over in excellent condition, cab clean, small soft coal, no large lumps. Fire made up with small coal, unable to get bar through before leaving. Firing then confined to front end until after Old Oak. Firing light, about four to five shovelfuls at a time. Riding very

Below: Shortly before this trip, No. 6000 King George V is seen approaching West Ruislip station working an up Shrewsbury express on 15 May 1962. (John Cramp)

rough, lot of vibration from the motion, but very free running. 90mph passing Haddenham, 70mph near Bicester. Engine worked very light for weight of train. Very noisy in cab and difficult to stand up at times. Had departed Paddington on time, 3min late passing High Wycombe, arrived Banbury 1min early, 60mph restriction at Fenny Compton; arrived Leamington 2min early, left Leamington on time, arrived Snow Hill 2min early.

Author's overview of these trips:

All engines were from Stafford Road (therefore often externally dirty in the last couple of years of service!) apart from No. 6000 which was an Old Oak Common engine. Journeys were subject to many signal stops and permanent way slacks which must have been very frustrating for the footplate crews, but the 'Kings' were easily capable of making up most if not all of the time lost, demonstrating their haulage power, acceleration, and overall fast running, even if not in the best of mechanical condition.

Above: From Dick Potts's observations, No. 6017 King Edward IV has probably not had a clean since it was seen in smart condition at Hatton with the 7.40am Birkenhead–Paddington express on 20 September 1961. (Michael Mensing)

1962–1967
BR finale and initial oblivion

February 1962 saw the withdrawal of the first 'King', No. 6006 *King George I*, which ironically was the one with the lowest recorded mileage (1,511,174 as against the highest, 1,950,462, achieved by No. 6013 *King Henry VIII*). However, it was to be another eight months before Swindon Works could bring itself to cut up the engine.

Extraordinarily, in the same month that No. 6006 was taken out of service, Swindon was overhauling and repainting No. 6025 *King Henry III*!

Right: Not a scene for the faint-hearted, No. 6006 King George I meets its end in Swindon Work's 'C' Shop. Withdrawn in February 1962, this depressing sight dates from 21 October 1962, with the engine reduced to its frames with the boiler being cut up separately alongside. (Mike Pope)

en more surprising was the outshopping
om Swindon Works, after an intermediate
erhaul, of No. 6002 *King William IV* as
te as June 1962, the same month that
w seven 'Kings' withdrawn. The engine
ppeared in resplendent condition although
e paintwork seemed to have been cleaned
ther than renewed, apart from the front

bufferbeam (not visible in the accompanying
view), which had been repainted.

When photographed at Swindon, No.
6002 was carrying an Old Oak Common
(81A) shedplate, but its last allocation was
to Stafford Road, Wolverhampton, and it
was withdrawn from there in September
1962. Perhaps it was originally intended to

be kept in reserve by Old Oak Common to
cover potential diesel failures, and then there
was a change of plan. As described later,
No. 6002 did enjoy a brief period of glory,
being put on display in early September
1962 at Birmingham Snow Hill station as a
farewell gesture to commemorate the end of
scheduled steam passenger operation on the

*Above: What a difference
just over a year makes! On
4 February 1962 No. 6025
King Henry III stands at
Swindon Works, having
just been overhauled
and repainted. At least
the Western Region then
obtained nearly 11 months
of use out of the locomotive
but, on 24 March 1963, it
is seen to have returned to
Swindon, this time to be
broken up there. (Bruce
Jenkins; Jim Oatway)*

*Left: The amazing sight of
a newly overhauled 'King',
No. 6002 King William IV,
at Swindon Works as late
as 3 June 1962, but with
only three months service
life remaining has to be
seen to be believed.
(Neil Davenport)*

*Right: No. 6002 King
William IV backs into
Swindon station for
a running-in turn on
17 June 1962, following
its futile overhaul.*
(Mike Pope)

*Right: No. 6000 King
George V, when based
at Bulmer's from 1968,
was not the first 'King'
to visit an engine shed
in Hereford. On 24 June
1962, Wolverhampton-
based No. 6022 King
Edward III was under
repair at the BR depot.*
(Geoff Rixon)

Birmingham line. Nevertheless, whether the work done on the locomotive at Swindon was money well spent, given that it provided barely three months of further service, is a moot point.

With a batch of withdrawals occurring in June and July it was clear that the 'Kings'' days were now numbered. They were also starting to be susceptible to failure and turned up at some unusual sheds for repairs. In July, No. 6022 *King Edward III*, allocated to Wolverhampton (Stafford Road) shed, was found at Hereford shed with part of its motion removed. The locomotive returned to work but was withdrawn in September and stored at Stafford Road until May 1963.

There were other strange visitors around this time. No. 6026 *King John* was noted receiving repairs to its wheel sets at Southall shed on 15 July 1962. Also, No. 6000 *King George V* turned up unexpectedly at Reading shed on 15 August. This latter event has been recorded in an article printed in the magazine, *Branchline*, produced by the Bytown Railway Society of Canada. For the benefit of Canadians, the 'Kings' are described as 'a powerful, high speed mainline machine in a small package'. The author of the article, most of which is reproduced opposite, is Colin Churcher. Colin took a holiday job at Reading shed while studying at Reading University and went on to become a management trainee with BR, Assistant Station Manager at Reading, and Area Manager, Haverfordwest, before emigrating to Canada in 1968 where he has become an authority on railway safety regulation.

Close encounter with a 'King' – by Colin Churcher

I was a cleaner at Reading in the summer of 1962. The diesels were already upon us and the 'Kings' would all be withdrawn by the end of the year. Reading was 36 miles west of London Paddington and the only 'Kings' we saw were non-stop, running through on the main line – until Wednesday, 15 August.

I signed on at 6am and made my way to the cleaners' room where everyone was excited because No. 6000 *King George V* was on shed. It had failed the previous night and was being made ready to run light engine to Swindon. We ran out and stood in awe of this machine which we regarded as the pinnacle of steam locomotion. It had a good coat of paint but was in need of a clean. At that moment, Eddie, the Chargehand Foreman, came out and we asked if we could clean the 'King'. He scowled and said: 'It's not one of ours but *Gladiator* will be going out this morning and that needs a wipe down.'

No. 5076 *Gladiator* was one of our 'Castles' and we always kept it in good condition. We argued with Eddie to no avail, although he did allow a couple of us to get out the Brasso and polish the King's bell.

As soon as Eddie had wandered off we got up on the footplate. The controls were almost identical to the later 'Castles'. One attractive feature of all former Great Western engines was the varnished hardwood handles on the valves. This encouraged care from the footplate crews – certainly not the rough treatment frequently meted out to locomotives from other regions where a stiff steam valve might be 'helped' with the coal pick.

Of course, once in the cab I had to put on a shovelful of coal. The firebox was very narrow as it was set above the rear driving wheels and between the wheels. To get coal to the front of the firebox one had to throw the coal about twelve feet. My shovelful hit the front tube plate with a satisfying clunk. I said to the others: 'See if you can throw the coal so hard that you can ring the bell'.

Everyone had a go and, although all but one hit the tube plate, none made the bell ring. The one who couldn't get the coal to the front was Titch. This short fellow, about 17 years old, intended to join the Grenadier Guards. He would have needed to have grown a lot to have reached their minimum height requirements.

There is a story that only one fireman was able to make the bell ring. He tied a thin wire to the bell, ran it back to the cab and tied it to a damper handle. When he made his swing he trod on the wire and rang the bell!

The fireman allocated to No. 6000 for its journey to Swindon arrived while we were engaged in putting coal to the front of the firebox. He was in ecstasy because he was actually going to fire on the 'King' and his driver had promised to let him drive. He was so elated that he wasn't even upset with us for putting way too much coal up front – the normal method of firing was to build a four or five foot deep fire at the back and the motion of the engine would normally move the fire forward to the front.

At that moment Eddie came by and we all scurried back to put the finishing touches to *Gladiator*. This engine had one thing in common with 'Kings' – a riveted tender. Some 'Castles' had welded (Hawksworth) flat-sided tenders which were much easier to clean. One had to clean around all of the rivets so working on the tender took much more time.

This was my only encounter with a 'King'. I saw the fireman a couple of days later. He was still on cloud nine after firing on this famous locomotive.

Left: Some three weeks after failing, No. 6000 King George V has clearly recovered and been cleaned, but not at Reading! It heads away from Old Oak Common towards North Acton with the 6.8pm Paddington–Wolverhampton train on 7 September 1962, the penultimate day of scheduled 'King' workings. (John Cramp)

Right: Earlier in 1962, No. 6026 King John storms up Saunderton Bank, where the up and down lines are separated, with the up 'Cambrian Coast Express'. (Nick Lera)

During the summer of 1962, despite their withdrawal from the London–South Wales services in March, 'Kings' were still operating many of the expresses on the Birmingham line.

They also helped out on expresses betwe[en] London and the West Country. Neverthele[ss] there were occasions when, in a desperate [bid] to find work for them, 'Kings' were unusual[ly] employed on more mundane duties. On 30 June 1962, just prior to its withdrawal, No. 6003 *King George IV* was noted on the down slow line at Reading working a fitted freigh[t.] 'Kings' were also seen hauling Didcot–Paddington semi-fasts in the morning rush hour, with No. 6000 *King George V* being use[d] on one such working on 13 August, as well as on other occasions.

The reign of the 'Kings' on scheduled express workings ceased on 8 September 1962 with the end of the summer timetab[le.]

Right: 'Kings' working local passenger trains, other than on running-in turns in the Swindon area, were a rare occurrence, but in summer 1962 they appeared on semi-fasts (all stations from Didcot to Reading and then fast to Paddington). On 8 August, No. 6019 King Henry V is seen leaving Pangbourne with the 8.10am from Didcot. (Ian Nash)

Left: A few weeks later,
No. 6000 King George V
was caught steaming
away from Pangbourne
with the 7.10am from
Didcot. How many
commuters realised they
were being honoured?
(Ian Nash)

Although occasional substitutions for failed
diesels occurred until the end of the year.
Throughout that summer the class had
continued to dominate passenger services
between Paddington and Birmingham/
Wolverhampton and Shrewsbury. By this
time there was an hourly daytime service
from Paddington to Birmingham as well
as additional peak hour trains, frequencies
having been increased from 1959 as a
result of electrification of the London
Midland Region's route to Birmingham,
requiring reduced running to facilitate the
engineering work.

The diversion of services from the
LMR to the Western Region resulted in
an increase in daily services via the direct
line to Birmingham from nine in each
direction to 14 up trains and 15 down
trains. Prior to the migration of services
from the LMR, the usage of 'Kings' and

Left: Looking as though
it is running along
a rural branch line,
No. 6012 King Edward VI
brings the 4.10pm
Paddington–Birkenhead
express across the fields
near Saunderton, where
the up line is some
distance away from the
down, on 5 June 1962.
(John Cramp)

'Castles' on the Western Region's Birmingham line was roughly equal, but the influx of additional services coincided with the withdrawal of 'Kings' from most of the West of England services, enabling more of this class to be available for the Birmingham line services, with 'Castles' being restricted to just two trains in each direction.

As a testament to their outstanding performance, 'Kings' worked express trains on this line from 1928 right through to September 1962 when diesels took over, a remarkable reign of 34 years. At the beginning of that month, to commemorate the demise of 'Kings' on

that route, No. 6002 *King William IV* was exhibited at Birmingham Snow Hill station, and had to be unexpectedly pressed into service on 4 September to substitute for a failed diesel.

As stated above, scheduled workings by 'Kings' ceased after Saturday, 8 September 1962. On that day, whether as a farewell gesture or as a means of moving the locomotive to Swindon for scrapping/disposal, the mid-afternoon milk train empties from West Ealing to Whitland, latterly a regular 'Castle' working, was seen on the main line at Southall hauled by a highly polished, unidentified 'King'. A few minutes earlier, No. 6019

King Henry V had passed by on an up express. On the following day, No. 6000 worked an enthusiasts' special from Wolverhampton to Swindon.

Before concentrating on their demise it is appropriate to recall the location which all members of the 'King' class regularly visited – Brunel's cathedral known as Paddington station (see picture opposite).

On 10 September, Nos 6002, 6010, 6020 and 6021 were lying out of use at Old Oak Common shed while No. 6018 was pottering around on empty carriage stock duties. On 30 September, four more 'Kings' were noted to have joined the

Below: Following its recent somewhat pointless overhaul at Swindon Works, No. 6002 King William IV briefly basks in glory while displayed at Birmingham Snow Hill on 4 September 1962. It was called on to replace a defunct diesel later in the same day.
(Bryan Hicks)

Left: Some four years after its outstanding achievements on the 'Bristolian', No. 6019 King Henry V stands at Paddington on 19 August 1962, hardly looking like an engine with less than one month of service left before withdrawal.
(Geoff Rixon)

Left: Paddington's famous arched roofs provide a classic backdrop to No. 6027 King Richard I as Hawksworth pannier tank No. 9420 prepares to leave with empty stock, on 7 May 1962.
(Great Western Trust collection)

Left and below: On 27 October 1962, No. 6011 King James I stands on the turntable at Newbury Racecourse while an inspector, intending to change the train reporting number from Z10 to Z12, holds the number 2, which he has just removed from No. 6000 King George V in the background. Then, after being turned, No. 6011, now designated Z12, is ready to return to the station to pick up its train for London. (Mike Pope)

withdrawn locomotives lying at Old Oak Common: Nos 6009, 6019, 6026 and 6029, but in contrast, No. 6000 was standing resplendent inside the roundhouse.

In all, 13 members of the class were taken out of service that month, adding to the eleven already withdrawn earlier in 1962. The survivors remained in case of diesel failures, a commonplace phenomenon, and to undertake any important random work that came along. On 29 September, No. 6000 had hauled a Talyllyn Railway special from Paddington to Ruabon (not the first visit by a 'King' to this location, but one requiring special authorisation nevertheless), and on its return, having hauled a Shrewsbury–Wolverhampton local, it assisted an

ailing diesel on the 6.40pm Shrewsbury–Paddington service instead of returning light engine to Old Oak Common.

The six 'Kings' remaining in service at the start of October were Nos 6000 *King George V*, 6005 *King George II*, 6011 *King James I*, 6018 *King Henry VI*, 6025 *King Henry III*, and 6028 *King George VI*. Known workings are detailed as follows. On 4 October No. 6000 worked the 5.30pm Paddington–Plymouth service as far as Exeter, and on 18 October No. 6005 hauled the 'Inter City' from Paddington to Shrewsbury, returning with the 'Cambrian Coast Express' as far as Birmingham, where No. 6011 took over. On 26 October, for the royal opening of a new steelworks at Llanwern, near Newport, Nos 6000 and

6018 hauled special trains containing VIPs from Paddington, although the Royal Train itself was diesel hauled. On the following day, No. 6000 was back in action hauling a Newbury race special, with two other race specials being hauled by Nos 6005 and 6011.

Finally that month, on the 30th, No. 6011 worked the 10am Birmingham–Paddington two-hour express.

There was still a little work to be found for the survivors in the following month. On 3 November, No. 6000 was recorded working the up 'Inter City' and on the17th, No. 6018 headed the LCGB's 'King Commemorative Rail Tour' from Paddington to Wolverhampton.

For a few days during November, Nos 6011

Above: No. 6011 King James I (leading) and No. 6018 King Henry VI apply their combined weight to the new northbound span of the rebuilt bridge over the River Wye at Chepstow on 5 November 1962. The town is visible behind No. 6018. (Great Western Trust collection)

Above left and right: With No. 7018 Dryslliwyn Castle standing alongside with a Newbury race special, No. 6000 King George V is also ready to leave Paddington for Newbury. The date is Friday, 23 November 1962 and, despite being only a couple of weeks from withdrawal, No. 6000 looks spotless, even down to the tender axle box covers, although the American medals on the cab side appear to be missing.
(Roy Hobbs)

Right: The weather on the last day of 'King'-hauled Newbury race specials, 24 November 1962, was particularly dull, as evident in this view of No. 6025 King Henry III approaching Twyford.
(John Beckett)

and 6018 were used for load tests on the Wye Bridge at Chepstow, which was in the course of being renewed.

Over the years, 'Kings' had been used several times for bridge tests, perhaps the most noteworthy being those carried out in March 1934 over six new relief line bridges installed for the quadrupling of the Birmingham line near the city. No fewer than four 'Kings' were used, running parallel in pairs at speeds of 60mph, with a total weight in excess of 500 tons. The locomotives in question were No. 6001 coupled to Nos 6014 and 6017 coupled to No. 6005, the latter pair hauling two carriages.

On 23 November, contrary to statements made in several other publications to the effect that 27 October marked the last 'King'-hauled Newbury race specials, No. 6000 worked one such train along with No. 7018 Drysllwyn Castle.

Then, on the following day, 24 November, Nos 6000 and 6025 had a final fling working these prestigious trains. This may well have been No. 6000's final passenger turn, for it was withdrawn during the week ending 4 December, leaving Nos 6011, 6018 and 6025 still available for service; Nos 6005 and 6028 having been withdrawn in November.

The last three operational survivors were all seen at work in December. No. 6011 worked the 10.50am Paddington–Plymouth parcels train on 14 December, No. 6025 headed the up 'Royal Duchy' on 17 December (so must have worked a down service prior to that), and No. 6018 hauled the 12.05pm Paddington–Penzance (but not into Cornwall), on 21 December. On the same day, No. 6011 worked the 10.50 from Paddington to Shrewsbury and returned to London with the relief 'Cambrian Coast Express' on the following day, 22 December, making this probably the last 'King'-hauled timetabled train.

Immediately after this trip, on 22 December 1962, No. 6011 was withdrawn, along with No. 6025, leaving No. 6018 as the sole survivor until its withdrawal at the end of the month, whereupon the class was now officially extinct. Rumours that the last four survivors, Nos 6000, 6011, 6018 and 6025, were to be retained in case they were needed for the 1963 Summer timetable sadly proved unfounded.

Left: No. 6025 King Henry III standing next to No. 6000 King George V at Newbury Racecourse station, ready to return to London. (John Beckett)

Below: Working what is thought to be the last 'King'-hauled timetabled service, No. 6011 King James I waits at Leamington Spa with the down relief 'Cambrian Coast Express' on 22 December 1962. The photographer was astounded and somewhat unprepared when the 'King' came into view instead of the expected diesel-hydraulic. (Bryan Hicks)

Right: The unusual sight of a local train hauled by a withdrawn express passenger locomotive is captured on film, as No. 6018 King Henry VI descends Hatton Bank on 22 April 1963, the first of four consecutive days of operation working the 6.05pm from Birmingham Snow Hill to Leamington Spa. (Bryan Hicks)

Below: No. 6018 King Henry VI waits at Birmingham Snow Hill to start its last revenue-earning journey. (John McCann/Online Transport Archive)

The final BR special

Withdrawal at the end of December 1962 for No. 6018 *King Henry VI*, was not quite the end. The locomotive was put in store at Old Oak Common shed and despatched to Swindon Works for attention in March 1963, emerging on 18 April, whereupon it was sent to Stafford Road shed (in error), and then to Tyseley the following day. Its smokebox number plate was removed and a GWR-style number applied to its front bufferbeam. The BR smokebox shed plate was also removed and the GWR shed code for Tyseley (TYS) painted on the front valance of the running plate.

The reason for all this attention was that No. 6018 was being reinstated into service for a farewell Stephenson Locomotive

Society 'King' special from Birmingham to Swindon via the Greenford loop and Southall, on 28 April 1963. Following its withdrawal the engine had been out of use for some four months so, in preparation for the final run, it was used between 22 and 25 April on the 6.5pm local train from Birmingham Snow Hill to Leamington, returning light engine to Tyseley.

The locomotive showed itself to be in fine fettle on 28 April, reaching speeds of 88mph at Blackthorn, near Bicester, on the outward journey, and 82mph at Uffington on the return trip via Oxford. The top speed achieved was on the down working at Denham. The noise of the locomotive as it approached Denham was so great that observers initially thought that the 'King' had failed and been replaced by a diesel – until No. 6018 roared through at 91mph! Furthermore, this was no lightweight train – the locomotive was hauling 440 tons, some 650 passengers being carried. In addition, there was only limited opportunity for fast running because the special was operated on a Sunday and there were several permanent way checks in force due to engineering works.

The weight of the train on the return journey up Hatton Bank could have proved problematic, particularly since speed had to be reduced to 37mph through Warwick, prior to the ascent, but No. 6018 managed to maintain 42mph on the 1-in-110 gradient. This compared extremely well with Pacific-hauled trains climbing steep banks on other regions, e.g. 57.5mph for a 'Duchess' on a mere 355 tons (full) and 48.5mph for an A4 hauling 365 tons (full). Bearing in mind the more modern cylinder designs of the Pacifics, enabling better steaming, and the age and size of the 'King', the performance of No. 6018 on 28 April 1963 was outstanding, resulting in this famous class going out in a blaze of glory.

In June 2010, fireman R.S. (Dick) Potts put together, partly from memory and partly from contemporaneous notes, the following account of this final passenger working of a 'King' in pre-preservation days:

"Sunday, 28 April, 1963, and the GWR "Kings" had all been withdrawn from

service in the previous year, but No. 6018 *King Henry VI* had been resurrected for this final trip organised by the Midland Area of the Stephenson Locomotive Society.

My regular driver, Albert Slater and myself, were rostered to work the special on its round trip from Birmingham Snow Hill to Swindon Works via High Wycombe, Greenford loop, Southall, Reading, Swindon, and return via Oxford and Banbury. The total mileage was about 285 miles.

On the Sunday morning, we found No. 6018 prepared and coaled with all sorts of "fuel", ranging from large and small ovoids, hard coal cobbles, lots of dust and even grass! The height of all this came only level with the top of the toolboxes in the tender. This meant that I was unable to build up the usual big fire to burn through gradually and the presence of quite a few "passengers" on the footplate prevented any shovelling. We took our train of 12 coaches (396 tons tare, 440 tons

gross) out of Tyseley sidings tender first to Snow Hill where some 650 enthusiasts boarded the carriages and the engine ran round the train, in readiness to depart.

Leaving Snow Hill with 250psi and a full glass of water I then had to fire fast and heavy in an attempt to gradually build up a shape in the firebox. However, No. 6018 steamed so well on this rubbish that all went well, especially as we were checked at Hatton and then stopped at Leamington Spa for water as all the troughs had been removed. A good climb was made to Claydon Crossing where we encountered single-line working to Cropredy. From here we accelerated well through Banbury at 50mph, Ardley at 63mph, Bicester at 81mph and Blackthorn at 88mph. A good climb to Saunderton was spoilt by a p/w man showing us a red flag, which we found out was to warn us of a defective signal at West Wycombe. We took water again at High Wycombe and from there

Above: During the gloomy part of the last day, No. 6018 King Henry VI pauses alongside Southall engine shed before drawing into the station to deposit its passengers for a visit to the shed. (Geoff Rixon)

accelerated away, with some rapid firing taking place, to pass Beaconsfield at 52mph From 180lb boiler pressure near Tyler's Green, pressure was soon restored to 240lb for the dash through Denham at 91mph.

We then took the Greenford loop to West Ealing and on to Southall where the enthusiasts visited the loco shed.

From here, a Southall driver was our pilotman to Reading as my driver did not know the road. I now had a very large fire in the box and we left with 250lb and a full glass. He was an excellent engineman and I had no problems on the run to Reading, where we again had to stop for water. The coal was now well back in the tender so I spent most of the time pulling the coal forward. We left Reading on the main line but at Pangbourne we went relief line to Didcot and then regained the main line on to Swindon.

Firing was now heavy and involved double shovelling, first from the back of the tender to the front, and then into the firebox. Consequently, I was unable to keep up the fire level but we did arrive at Swindon only a few minutes late.

During the lay-over at Swindon, No. 6018 was taken to the shed for servicing.

We then returned to our train with a mountain of hard cobbles in the tender and a large fire made up of the same. From here, with the permission of my driver and the loco inspector, I did the driving to Oxford. The firing was done by a fellow fireman from Tyseley, Bernard Rainbow, so steam and water was no problem. An ROS of 50mph was on at Marston and once over that we roared away to pass Uffington at 82mph, but had to slow down then to go on the relief line from Challow to Wantage Road. After a burst of speed to 74mph at Milton, we then progressed slowly around Foxhall curve and on to Oxford. Here, I retired to the train and left Bernard to face Hatton Bank.

Even after a signal check at Warwick, Hatton was passed in 9min from Leamington at 42mph. From then on steaming was very poor and No. 6018 was eased along to Tyseley. Here, I returned to the footplate and on arriving at Snow Hill found the cause of the poor steaming. The smokebox door was red hot at the bottom

causing air to be drawn in and burning the smokebox ash. We then took the train back to Tyseley carriage sidings and put No. 6018 on shed to "cool down".

The locomotive was in superb condition – very smooth riding and quiet. Apart from the last part of the journey from Hatton, steaming was marvellous.

A couple of days later, No. 6018 went light engine to Swindon on its final journey.'

Even after its brief stay of execution for this final run, it seemed that No. 6018 might yet escape the cutter's torch. Rumours abounded that the locomotive was to swop identities with the preservation candidate, the iconic No. 6000 *King George V*, which reputedly was suffering from a cracked frame, but there is no evidence that a substitution ever took place. More plausible is the story that the locomotive was to be purchased by Butlins for static display at one of their holiday camps. Indeed, in July 1963, the locomotive was reported to be inside Swindon Works being prepared for this acquisition, and it is believed that restoration work had in fact commenced.

Unfortunately, the sale never materialised,

Right: Old Oak Common depot seemed reluctant to send its 'Kings' to be scrapped because as late as 19 October 1963, the date of these photographs, the two pictured here had been withdrawn for eleven months. With their once immaculate green paintwork still visible, No. 6005 King George II (missing its smokebox door handle), and No. 6028 King George VI, which the author subsequently found lying at Southall, await their fate.
(Geoff Rixon)

apparently because Swindon insisted on undertaking (and charging for) a full overhaul even though the locomotive was not intended for subsequent operation. Crewe Works, on the other hand, was content to carry out a more economical cosmetic job on their own locomotives, which was all that Butlins wanted. Whatever the truth, Butlins bought four LMS express locomotives and No. 6018 was cut up in October 1963, being one of ten 'Kings' to suffer this indignity at its birthplace, instead of being sold to scrap merchants.

While No. 6018 found itself in limbo the remaining members of the class, excluding No. 6000, were prepared for their final journeys to the scrapyards or for cutting up at Swindon. Initially, some were stored at depots such as Old Oak Common and Stafford Road (Wolverhampton) before gravitating to Swindon. The author recalls photographing No. 6028 in temporary storage at Southall shed after it had been towed there by No. 7923 *Speke Hall* from Old Oak Common, together with Nos 2842 and 4705, on 5 January 1964, the 'King' having been withdrawn more than a year

earlier. The sight of these fine locomotives languishing out of use and rusting in the open air was very depressing, particularly since so many members of the class had been kept in superb external condition right to the end, their former cleanliness still visible as the elements gradually took hold.

The scrapping of No. 6018 *King Henry VI* was particularly regrettable, since it had several claims to fame. As well as being BR's last operational 'King', outliving the rest of the class by four months and performing magnificently on the farewell special on 28 April 1963, it had also been selected to represent the Western Region in the 1948 Locomotive Exchanges. Furthermore, for the benefit of those sceptics who doubt that No. 3440 *City of Truro* reached 102.3mph, No. 6018 had provided the first fully authenticated record of a GWR engine exceeding (as opposed to reaching) 100mph when it achieved 102.5mph on a down 'Bristolian' working in 1954. In that same year, on 1 July, No. 6018 had worked the 50th anniversary running of the 'Cornish Riviera Express'. On the downside, it had come close to losing a driving wheel at high speed.

Yet, due to an unlikely turn of events, there was some compensation for the loss of No. 6018. Two 'Kings' destined for the scrapyard were spared, No. 6023 *King Edward II* and No. 6024 *King Edward I*. Both were initially sold to Messrs T.W. Ward of Briton Ferry, who, like other scrap merchants, apart from Woodhams, would have broken up the engines almost immediately. However, when BR realised that 'Kings' were banned west of Cardiff (which they were at that time) the engines could not be delivered to Briton Ferry by rail, so the sale to Wards was cancelled.

Instead, they were re-sold to Woodham Bros at Barry and, as is generally well known, this scrap merchant concentrated on breaking up wagons, while leaving over 200 steam locomotives intact. The subsequent removal by BR of a 'no-resale' clause in its contract with Woodhams enabled this vast quantity of engines to be saved. Barry was also west of Cardiff, but BR were prepared to allow Nos 6023 and 6024 to be taken this short distance (some ten miles) beyond there. Of course, no-one at that time could have imagined that these locomotives would escape the cutter's torch.

Left: Together yet again, and not for the last time! No. 6023 King Edward II stands in front of No. 6024 King Edward I in the yard at Swindon Works on 21 October 1962. Cross heads and bottom slide bars have been cut through and are lying on the ground in readiness for the locomotives to be towed to South Wales for intended scrapping. On the right is No. 6008 King James II, which was broken up at Swindon. (Mike Pope)

Below: One could be forgiven for thinking that the front number plate has been put on a different 'King', but this rusty heap photographed at Swindon Works on 20 September 1964 really is the famous flagship locomotive, No. 6000 King George V. Positive proof is provided by the lower positioning of the double-red route restriction circles on the cabside resulting from the location of the American medallions. Preserved Taff Vale Railway Class 01 No. 28 (GWR No. 450) is in the background. (Michael Allen)

Extraordinarily, the flagship locomotive, No. 6000, took on the same appearance, if not worse, as the rest of the withdrawn members of the class. Given that it was on the list of locomotives to be preserved for the Nation, one would have expected it to have been cared for following its withdrawal, but this was not so. It was dumped at Swindon Works while its future was debated and was then towed to Stratford Works in East London in Autumn 1964 to join other locomotives earmarked for preservation.

The intention was that No. 6000 would be restored and placed in Clapham Museum in London, where its nameplates, cab side number plates, bell and medallions had already been sent. The decision was then taken to close the museum and move the existing exhibits, which included several steam locomotives, elsewhere. However, Swindon Museum expressed an interest in taking No. 6000 and placing it in proposed additional accommodation. As a result, the engine was brought back to Swindon on 31 December 1966. It was put in the Stock Shed, from where, some 2½ years later, this phoenix would miraculously rise from the ashes.

1968–2011
Royal renaissance

Following its return from Stratford Works on 31 December 1966, as a result of its planned restoration and display being abandoned through economic cut-backs, No. 6000 was stored under cover in Swindon Work's Stock Shed. This was pending implementation of a revised plan to restore and display the engine in an enlarged Swindon Museum, there being no space in the existing premises for such a large exhibit without removing one or two existing locomotives. However, the enlargement plan was then put on ice, resulting in No. 6000 remaining in the Stock Shed, rusting and gathering dust. Before long, the railway tracks leading to the shed were removed. The engine, which nobody seemed to want, was now marooned and forgotten.

Right: No. 6000 King George V is just about to leave the Swindon Stock Shed on 9 August 1968, where it has been stored for some 18 months following its return from Stratford Works. The engine has been cleaned up and its regalia (medals, name and number plates) replaced. (Author)

Bulmer to the rescue

Salvation for No. 6000 came unexpectedly and from a surprising source. H.P. Bulmer Ltd, the Hereford-based cider makers, had a problem. Large numbers of guests and visitors came to their factory to view the cider-making processes, but there were no suitable visitor reception facilities on site and little room to build any. As the factory had a rail connection with BR, the company hit upon an idea for solving the problem – they would purchase some redundant, prestigious railway carriages and use these instead, parking them on a siding within the site, and perhaps even taking them out on tour as a travelling exhibition train. So it was that Bulmers approached BR, resulting in the purchase of five Pullman cars which had previously been part of the 'Golden Arrow' set.

Bulmer's Group Managing Director, Peter Prior, had been instrumental in purchasing the Pullman cars and was something of a latent enthusiast, having been a trainspotter in his childhood. While driving to London one day, he picked up a hitch-hiker and in conversation with him,

Left: With the Mayor and Mayoress of Swindon, together with Peter Prior of Bulmers, standing on the running plate of the locomotive, people power drags No. 6000 from the Stock Shed in the pouring rain on 9 August 1968. Time for another pint of cider! (Author)

mentioned the purchase of the Pullman cars. The hitch-hiker expressed surprise that a steam locomotive was not being acquired to haul these carriages and said that he knew of a suitable one, No. 6000 *King George V*, telling Peter of the engine's location and current misfortunes.

As a result of this conversation, Peter Prior set about establishing the locomotive's status and was surprised to find that it was leased by BR to Swindon Corporation and that the custodian was the Borough Librarian! Peter was allowed to inspect No. 6000 in the Stock Shed on 21 March 1968, following which he was able to negotiate a sub-lease to Bulmers for an initial period of two years (later extended), subject to the company looking after it and returning it to running order.

The next stage was for Bulmers to find a contractor to overhaul No. 6000. Hunslet in Leeds were provisionally earmarked

to undertake the work, until BR quoted a fee of £10,000 to tow the locomotive from Swindon to Leeds and then to Hereford. This high fee prompted Bulmers to look for a contractor closer to hand and they settled on A.R. Adams & Son of Newport, saving approximately £3,500 in transportation costs.

Adams were used to repairing colliery engines for the National Coal Board, but despite never having overhauled such a large locomotive as No. 6000 before, they carried out an excellent restoration of the locomotive to working order. Due to the removal of rail access at Adam's site, the work was actually carried out at the nearby premises of the United Wagon Company.

Having found a restoration contractor, Bulmers now needed stewards to look after and maintain No. 6000 once it had arrived at Hereford. Contact was made with the Great Western Society, which formed a Hereford Group virtually overnight

from a nucleus of society members living in that area. The author was serving on the society's management council at the time and well remembers the excitement which this approach generated. The inaugural meeting of the Hereford Group was held on 5 July 1968 when the locomotive's nameplates, number plates, medallions and bell (just one at this stage!) were handed over to the society. After a couple of years, however, it was clear that the activities of the Hereford Group, which were naturally focussed on the wellbeing of No. 6000 and its relationship with Bulmers, would be better carried out separately from the Great Western Society. At this time the GWS was concentrating on securing and developing Didcot shed as a permanent home for the society's scattered stock. So it was that the Hereford Group parted company with the GWS and became the 6000 Locomotive Association.

The final piece of the jigsaw was the extraction of No. 6000 from the Swindon Stock Shed to enable it to be towed to Newport for restoration into operational condition. However, as mentioned previously, the trackwork linking the shed with the remainder of the works network, approximately 300 yards in length, had been lifted. Consequently, Bulmers paid a contractor to lay a temporary section of track to enable No. 6000 to be hauled out of the shed, whereupon BR informed Bulmers that they would not allow one of their diesel shunters on to this new section of track because they had not been responsible for laying it. This prompted Bulmers to place an advertisement in the Personal Column of *The Times* requesting 2,000 volunteers to come to Swindon Works on Friday, 9 August 1968 to pull No. 6000 manually over the 300 yards of unapproved track.

Despite the fact that many railway enthusiasts were heading northwards around this time to witness the last steam operations on BR two days later (or so everyone thought at the time), there was no shortage of manpower to rescue No. 6000. Drenched by pouring rain and quenched by copious amounts of Bulmer's cider, the author was one such volunteer who took a day's leave from work and found himself grabbing one of the ropes attached to the front of the locomotive – when not taking photographs of this extraordinary event! No. 6000 had already been cleaned up for the occasion and was wearing its regalia (number plates, nameplates, medallions and bell). The hand shunt proved successful and the locomotive was dragged to the waiting diesel, No. D4123.

The engine's restoration and return to working order took a remarkably short time owing to the fact that it was in better mechanical condition than expected. In the middle of the night of Wednesday/Thursday 30/31 October 1968, so that no-one could witness the horror of a steam engine being on the main line, No. 6000 was towed in light steam from Newport to Hereford, arriving at the break of dawn. The official launch of the exhibition train in Bulmer's sidings took place on Wednesday 13 November after which, for what was almost three years, No. 6000 was confined to steaming up and down these sidings – a caged lion separated from the outside world of BR by a mere wire fence.

However, an immediate extension of the sidings at least enabled *King George V* to make trips of about one mile, and on 29 March 1969 the first visit by a BR train (a DMU) was made direct into Bulmer's site. At least, enthusiasts could have a ride behind No. 6000 on the various open days and special visits that Bulmer and the Great Western Society organised at the Bulmer Railway Centre, and many people regarded this as infinitely preferable to the locomotive being mounted on a plinth in a static museum such as Clapham or Swindon.

Below: The magnificent caged lion, carrying a Hereford shed plate, stands in Bulmers sidings with former 'Golden Arrow' Pullman carriages on 22 March 1970. (Author)

Breaking the steam ban

The running of the final steam specials in the North West of England on 11 August 1968 marked the end of standard gauge main line steam on BR. In an attempt to brainwash the public into thinking of BR only in terms of a modern diesel and electric rail network, steam was meant to be banished from sight permanently. The only steam locomotives to break this ban were the Great Western Society's 0-4-2 tank No. 1466 and Alan Pegler's LNER A3 Pacific *Flying Scotsman*.

No. 1466 operated an auto train service on the Cholsey to Wallingford branch (then still in use by BR for freight), on 21 September 1968, arrangements having been initiated before the announcement of the steam ban. As for *Flying Scotsman*, the owner, Alan Pegler, had the foresight to enter into a contract with BR for its continued operation and this remained the only standard gauge steam locomotive to be allowed to work on BR until its final passenger trip on 31 August 1969, after which it was shipped to America to go on tour.

Occasional chinks in the steam ban did appear between 1969 and 1971. For example, Great Western Society locomotives were invited to give passenger rides at BR open days at Reading and St Blazey, and No. 1466 was allowed to operate on BR metals for a film contract (*Young Winston*) on the former Neath & Brecon Railway near Craig-y-nos in South Wales. However, the engines were always piloted by a diesel on the main line. Although these and other operations were regarded at the time as minor achievements, they were nothing compared with what was to come.

The key date which led to the surprising relaxation of the main line steam ban was 8 March 1971. On this date the annual Royal Command Film Performance was held at the Odeon Cinema, Leicester Square, in London, in the presence of HRH The Queen Mother. The main film, *Love Story*, was preceded by a documentary made by the National Coal Board in 1969, which included footage of No. 6000 in steam at Bulmers. Peter Prior was in the

audience and had brought a guest, William Thorpe, Deputy Chairman of BR, who was clearly impressed by the sight of No. 6000. Peter took his guest to dinner after the film performance and asked him for permission to run the locomotive on the main line. On the following day, William Thorpe rang Peter to inform him that the BR Board was prepared to consider allowing No. 6000 on the main line as a one-off experiment, to establish how practical it was to operate steam on a modern diesel/electric rail network. Months of negotiations then ensued, with the BRB finally agreeing to the proposal on 8 September 1971.

Urgent preparations were now made for the long-awaited steam-hauled exhibition train tour to venture on to the main line at the beginning of October 1971. A supposedly secret trial run of No. 6000 between Hereford and Newport with the locomotive hauling a single BR coach, took place successfully on 15 September, after which the five Bulmer Pullman carriages were then trialled.

The stage was now set for the week-long tour which took place between 2 and 9 October in four stages: October 2 – Hereford–Birmingham (Tyseley) via Severn Tunnel and Oxford; October 4 – Birmingham (Moor St) to Kensington (Olympia); October 7 – Olympia to Swindon and October 9 – Swindon to Hereford via Bath, Bristol (Stapleton Road) and Severn Tunnel Junction. The five Pullmans were supplemented by some standard BR coaches, so No. 6000 was hauling around 350 tons (full).

The tour was an unqualified success and thousands of people, including the author who nipped off from work, came to watch the exhibition train pass by. Apart from those people who had been lucky enough to see *Flying Scotsman* hauling a railtour between 12 August 1968 and 31 August 1969, spectators were seeing a steam-hauled train on the main line for the first time in over three years, with no guarantee they would ever see one again.

Above: Having been piloted on the main line by a diesel after attending a BR Open Day at St. Blazey, GWR Saddletank No. 1363 is pictured at Bodmin Road (now Bodmin Parkway) on 3 May 1970 with the former Glyncorrwg carriages, Nos 3755 and 3756. A diesel multiple unit on a local service can be seen lurking in the background. (Les Folkard)

Above: The first standard gauge steam-hauled passenger train on main line BR for two years is seen near Tackley, between Oxford and Banbury, heading for Birmingham (Tyseley) on 2 October 1971, hauled by No. 6000 King George V.
(John Beckett)

The BR locomotive inspector in charge of the tour was very complimentary about No. 6000, stating that it had performed admirably and was a great credit to all those responsible for its restoration and upkeep. Over the week, the engine travelled some 525 miles on 12 tons of coal and about 15,000 gallons of water.

Following the phenomenal interest taken in this tour by the public and the fact that no problems had arisen with running No.

6000, BR recognised that the steam ban was unwarranted and agreed to limited steam running from 1972. Owners were invited to nominate engines to be included on a list of approved engines potentially able to operate on BR, a list which initially was not confined to express passenger types, and included some unlikely candidates.

The list has been refined over the years and many additional restrictions and requirements have been imposed on

steam running (although there have been relaxations in other areas such as designate lines and top speed). However, the importan point is that, as a result of Bulmer's/Peter Prior's persistence, culminating in No. 6000 pioneering success in 1971, steam running has become a permanent fixture, with no current plans for its withdrawal. No. 6000 *King George V* was the engine that started the driving wheels running, giving this iconic locomotive another claim to fame.

Left: On its way from Birmingham Moor Street to Kensington Olympia on 4 October 1971, the Bulmers special arrives at High Wycombe station, watched by a large number of spectators including local school children who were taken to see this wonderful spectacle. BR allowed the crowd to gather on the running lines as the fire brigade prepared to replenish the locomotive's water tank. (Michael Furnell)

Above: On the fourth and final leg of its inaugural exhibition tour, No. 6000 passes Ponthir, north of Newport, on its way to Hereford via Pontypool and Abergavenny on 9 October 1971. (Author's collection)

Right: No. 6000's pioneering tour with the Bulmers exhibition train in October 1971 resulted in the lifting of the BR main line steam ban, imposed in August 1968. Unimaginable back then were operations such as the one which took place on 15 July 1973 when the Great Western Society ran special services to celebrate the centenary of the Bourne End to Marlow branch using Prairie tank No. 6106 (seen here being inspected at Maidenhead), 'Modified Hall' No. 6998 Burton Agnes Hall, and 0-4-2T No. 1450 (deputising for No. 1466). (Michael Furnell)

We three 'Kings'

By the mid-1960s only three 'Kings' still existed, the remaining 27 either having been broken up by external scrap merchants or by BR at Swindon Works. Those three still survive today, so it is now opportune to review their recent history and current status. No. 6000 has already been covered in depth up to and including the week-long exhibition tour in October 1971, so this section will merely cover this locomotive's later career while concentrating on the restoration of the two which emerged from Barry scrapyard, Nos 6023 and 6024.

Right: Hauling a Great Western Society railtour on 24 June 1973, No. 6000 passes Stokesay Castle, near Craven Arms, on its way from Hereford to Shrewsbury. The assorted carriages include two of the society's restored Collett vehicles at the rear, two Bulmer Pullman cars at the front, and a BR Gresley buffet car in the centre of the train. (Author's collection)

No. 6000 *King George V* (from 1972 onwards)

'KGV', as it has often been called, spent the next 15 years running on the main line, mostly with unqualified success but, as with all elderly working steam locomotives, there were some disappointments and a few mishaps along the way.

The worst incident involving No. 6000 took place on 6 September 1974, but not due to engine failure. The locomotive was on its way from Hereford to Swindon for the Works Open Day when its safety valve studs struck an overbridge at Lower Pontnewydd, near Cwmbran. The brass safety valve cover was torn off, later being found in a mangled state in a nearby field, but far more seriously, the safety valve itself was ripped out, causing a massive plume of steam to rise into the air with a tremendous noise. Fortunately, a manned police car happened to be parked within sight of the accident. The officers called the Fire Brigade who arrived within minutes and pumped water into the engine, thereby minimising damage and preventing an explosion.

Luckily, no permanent damage was done to the engine and it was repaired within a week. The cause of this potential disaster was the re-ballasting of the track which had reduced the clearance under this bridge. As a consequence, the 'King' was banned from running between Hereford and Newport although, for a special 50th birthday present, BR did allow No. 6000 a one-off trip along the line in 1977, hauling the Severn Valley Railway's vintage train composed of GWR stock. The locomotive's half-century was also marked by the creation of a limited-edition commemorative plaque which enthusiasts were able to purchase.

In January 1979, No. 6000 made the first of several visits to Swindon Works for work to be carried out. This initial visit, caused by the running of a hot axle box in October 1978, involved the removal of wheels to enable work to be carried out on the axles and boxes. However, hot box problems persisted and No. 6000 was back in Swindon Works in March 1979 for rectification, following which it resumed railtour duty.

Later in 1979, No. 6000's seven-year boiler certificate came up for renewal, necessitating the replacement of some tubes, and this was followed by a full repaint which was completed by early October 1980. The following year was

Right: The well-known transport photographer, Geoff Rixon, is the owner of one of the limited-edition plaques produced in 1977 to commemorate No. 6000's half-century. (Author's collection)

Opposite: Following repairs at Swindon Works, No. 6000 was displayed there in all its regal magnificence for the Works open day on 19 May 1979. (Peter Zabek)

KING GEORGE V GOLDEN JUBILEE

1927   1977

THIS PLAQUE IS N° 414 OF A LIMITED ISSUE OF 1,000 PRODUCED TO CELEBRATE THE JUBILEE OF THIS FAMOUS LOCOMOTIVE BUILT AT SWINDON FOR THE G.W.R., IT WENT TO THE FAIR OF THE IRON HORSE IN BALTIMORE U.S.A IN 1927 AND UNITS RETURN WORKED ALMOST 2,000,000 MILES BEFORE WITHDRAWAL FROM SERVICE IN 1962. REFURBISHED IN 1968, THE LOCOMOTIVE IS NOW OPERATED IN CONJUNCTION WITH B.R. BY BULMERS CIDER CO. HEREFORD

a busy one for the locomotive, but in early 1982 a boiler examination revealed that firebox repairs were needed. This necessitated the removal of the boiler from the frames for the first time since BR days. With agreement having been given by the National Railway Museum and Thamesdown District Council (successors to Swindon Corporation) to Bulmer's sub-lease being extended to 1987, No. 6000 was towed to Swindon Works in January 1983 for repairs to the boiler and firebox. These were completed in time for a railtour on 12 June. Remarkably, while the locomotive was in the works, members of the 6000 Locomotive Association were allowed access to paint the frames.

After more than a year of trouble-free running, the locomotive's tender started to develop hot box problems and this culminated in the engine visiting Swindon Works once again, after initially receiving attention at one of its former depots, Bristol (Bath Road). No. 6000 arrived at Swindon in late April 1985. Unfortunately, the engine's presence at Swindon coincided with the decision to close the works and repairs to the tender temporarily ceased. It was nearly four months after arriving at Swindon Works that No. 6000 departed, its destination being Cardiff (Canton) where the tender wheels were turned. It was not until 12 August 1985 that the locomotive was at last able to return to Hereford and resume main line duties, with some trips taking place in the latter part of the year.

However, work was scarce in 1986, with only one outing, and in 1987 the boiler certificate expired, as did the sub-lease at the end of the year, this having been extended by 12 months.

The 6000 Locomotive Association started to raise funds for the engine's next overhaul and contributions had reached around £35,000 when a bombshell dropped. The sub-lease was not being renewed and the locomotive moved to Swindon for static display. It has remained inoperable ever since and is currently being exhibited at the National Railway Museum (NRM), York.

The 6000 Locomotive Association has been disbanded and it is most unlikely that the locomotive will return to steam in the foreseeable future, for two reasons. First, there are now two other 'Kings' (Nos 6023 and 6024) available for main line work and, secondly, modifications to No. 6000 would have to be made to enable it to run on the national network, therefore arguably detracting too much from its originality, given its unique history.

Right: As the sun sets on King George V, while the locomotive stands on Didcot's turntable during the enthusiasts' gala weekend on 28/29 September 1985, so it would shortly be setting on No. 6000's operational career. No, your eyes are not deceiving you: the cab is slightly skewed, a peculiarity visible on the fireman's side, which remains unexplained to this day. (Author)

No. 6024 *King Edward I*

This locomotive was built at Swindon Works at a cost of £7,500 and entered service at Plymouth (Laira) shed on 5 July 1930. From there it moved to Newton Abbot in 1934 and stayed at that depot until 1948 when it returned to Laira. A transfer to Old Oak Common occurred in 1954 where it remained until 1961, at which time it moved to its final shed, Cardiff (Canton).

No. 6024 received its new boiler with four-row superheater in September 1953, and its double chimney in 1957. Following these modifications No. 6024 became a fast machine and was recorded attaining 101.5mph on Dauntsey Bank while working the 'Bristolian' in 1957, and 102mph while working the 'Cambrian Coast Express' near Denham in the early 1960s.

The locomotive was withdrawn in June 1962, having worked a total of 1,570,015 miles, and was dispatched from Canton to Swindon.

Instead of being broken up there, it was sold to Woodham Bros at Barry Docks in South Wales, as mentioned earlier, after sale to T.W. Ward had fallen through. The connecting rods and piston rods were cut through at Swindon to facilitate its being towed to the scrapyard. However, unlike other yards which cut up locomotives almost as soon as they arrived, Woodhams concentrated on breaking up goods wagons and left the steam locomotives to rust in the sea air, with the prospect of some of the metal content appreciating in value.

With more than 200 locomotives extant on site, Woodham's scrapyard became a magnet for railway enthusiasts, some of whom were anxious to purchase engines. Once Woodhams had obtained BR's agreement to rescind the no-resale clause, the engines could be bought by preservation groups, with the first one, an ex-Midland Railway Fowler 0-6-0, No. 43924, leaving in 1968. The early departures were chosen for their better condition or rarity. No. 6024 was regarded as being in poor condition, particularly with so many parts having

Above: No. 6024 King Edward I looks particularly smart as it hauls the 2.35pm Birkenhead–Paddington express between Solihull and Widney Manor on 8 September 1959. (Michael Mensing)

Left: Shortly after its arrival from Cardiff (Canton), No. 6024 King Edward I stands in the reception area at Swindon Works yard on 19 August 1962. In front of No. 6024 is No. 6023 King Edward II and beyond that stands the record-breaking locomotive, No. 4086 Builth Castle, the first Great Western engine to have reached an authenticated speed of 100mph since City of Truro's achievement in 1904. (Ian Nash)

Opposite: Even after restoration to working order, regular repairs and maintenance are necessary to keep an engine operational. Inside the Lifting Shop at Didcot shed on 17 May 2008, No. 6024 is hoisted up to enable the front bogie assembly to be refitted after the wheels had been sent to the Severn Valley Railway to be turned. (Frank Dumbleton/ Great Western Society)

Below: Illustrating the primitive working conditions endured by the restoration team when the locomotive first arrived at Quainton Road, the boiler of No. 6024 King Edward I rests on wooden blocks, having been lifted by crane from the frames, which are covered by a tarpaulin. (Mike Pope)

been removed or damaged, and as there was a 'King' already preserved (No. 6000) and working on the main line, No. 6024 was not considered a priority for saving.

Fortunately, there were some optimists about and in 1972 the King Preservation Society was formed to secure No. 6024. Following the success of an appeal for funds the engine and tender were bought for £4,250, and left Barry at the end of March 1973 for Quainton Road (now the Buckinghamshire Railway Centre), being the 36th hulk to escape from the South Wales yard. Some components had been taken from No. 6024 for use on No. 6000, e.g. the chimney, and as sister locomotive, No. 6023, was deemed to be totally beyond redemption following the cutting through of its rear driving wheels, No. 6023's chimney was purchased for No. 6024, along with other useful parts. It is interesting to note that, while No. 6000 carries some parts from No. 6024, so the latter consists of a major part which used to belong to No. 6000 – its boiler! Built

in 1953 with four-row superheater, this boiler had been transferred to No. 6024 in June 1960 when this engine received its last heavy overhaul at Swindon.

While the purchase of No. 6024 from Woodhams was nearing completion, the society had to find a suitable site where the locomotive could be restored. Most of the established preserved railways were based on branch lines, which were unable to take the weight of a 'King' class locomotive, and in the end, the society decided that No. 6024 should be taken to Quainton Road, even though no covered accommodation could be provided.

Following the locomotive's arrival on 1 April 1973, the first job was to dismantle it, a task which was completed in July 1974. Until July 1986, when covered accommodation became available, all the dismantling and restoration work had to be undertaken outside in all weathers, with nothing more than a rudimentary shelter made from tarpaulins and plastic sheeting for protection. It is a remarkable

achievement that the King Preservation Society, which later became the 6024 Preservation Society, was able to carry out what at that time was one of steam preservation's most formidable projects, in such dire conditions.

Following dismantlement, restoration progress started slowly due to lack of funds. Initially, efforts were concentrated on the tender which was suffering from extensive corrosion and also required re-wheeling. One of the main obstacles to the engine being returned to working order was the lack of connecting rods and piston rods, which had been removed to facilitate towing of the engine to Barry. It was therefore a major achievement when the society had raised enough money by 1982 to have new ones manufactured. Many more missing or damaged parts also had to be made, while others which had survived but had spent some ten years deteriorating in the sea air at Barry, such as the coupling rods, were renovated to remove rust and pitting. Some items were sent to Swindon Works for re-machining.

A milestone date in the restoration of No. 6024 was 20 March 1983, when the locomotive was re-wheeled. This involved the hire of two cranes to lift the frames and place them on to the renovated wheelsets. This was a complicated operation which was sufficiently newsworthy to make it into the following day's *Daily Telegraph* newspaper.

By this time, work had already started on the boiler and firebox which, due to cost considerations, had received little attention at Quainton Road during the 1970s. A new front tubeplate was manufactured to replace the existing one which was cracked and the laborious task of removing most of the boiler tubes and firebox stays and inserting new ones was underway. The society had hoped to have the engine in steam by 1985, the 150th anniversary of the GWR, but the amount of work to be carried out on the boiler and firebox, combined with limited financial resources, saw this target date slip by. Eventually, the society decided to contract out the remainder of the boiler work, in early 1987, by which

time another major event had occurred – the locomotive now had covered accommodation for the remainder of its restoration.

More milestones quickly followed. The boiler was successfully tested and reunited with the remainder of the locomotive on 28 March 1988, an event which was again covered by the *Daily Telegraph* and also by TV. Then, on 2 February 1989, came the moment everyone had been waiting for: No. 6024 in steam and running up and down the yard. On 26 April 1989, the locomotive was formally re-commissioned and 're-named' by HRH The Duke of Gloucester. The occasion generated more media attention and both the society and the public at large could now witness the fruits of the 16-year restoration, 12 of which had been carried out in extremely difficult conditions as a result of the work having to be undertaken in the open air.

Following the resolution of minor teething problems arising during the engine's operation within the Buckinghamshire Railway Centre site later in 1989, No. 6024 was ready to venture on to BR metals, running to Derby on 30 January 1990 for weighing and adjustment to springs. It then hauled a test train to Tyseley and Banbury two days later. The locomotive hauled its first passenger-carrying train in April 1990.

Having cost in the region of £200,000 to be returned to working order (a mere bagatelle compared with No. 6023 later!), No. 6024 has now enjoyed many years of main line running and visits to railway centres, punctuated by withdrawal in 1995 and 2002 for the regulatory overhauls required for continued service. The engine has proved to be a popular and reliable performer. Its crowning glory was probably on 10 June 2008 when it hauled the Royal Train carrying TRH The Prince of Wales and the Duchess of Cornwall over the Severn Valley Railway, with the Prince of Wales having a stint at driving. This followed the tradition set by his mother, HM The Queen, and his great grandfather, King George V, both of whom had driven 'Castle' class locomotives on visits to Swindon Works.

No. 6024's boiler 'ticket' is due to expire shortly and the 'King' baton for main line operation will therefore pass to No. 6023 for a time. At the end of 2010, financial problems (including litigation costs using up the funds required for No. 6024's impending costly overhaul) forced the 6024 Preservation Society to sell the engine. However, this cloud could have a silver lining because the new purchaser is the Royal Scot Locomotive and General Trust, which is well placed to fund No. 6024's overhaul and which has agreed that the 6024 Preservation Society can continue to maintain and operate the locomotive.

One hesitates to mention No. 6024's operational nadir but it was of considerable significance, having implications for all three surviving 'Kings' as far as main line running is concerned. No blame attaches to the locomotive or its operatives for the incident which occurred; it was simply a repetition of the calamity that beset No. 6000: re-ballasted track bringing the locomotive into contact with an overbridge. The fateful day was 22 March 1992 when No. 6024 was hauling the return 'William Shakespeare' special from Stratford upon Avon to London. About a mile and a half from Paddington, after being switched from the up relief to the up main line due to engineering work, the locomotive hit the girder of an overbridge at Ladbroke Grove, dislodging the safety valves and associated fittings and wrecking the brass safety valve cover. Luckily, the footplate crew was able to maintain boiler pressure by injecting more water into the boiler while beginning to drop the fire, and the emergency services were once again very quickly on the scene. A disaster was therefore averted and No. 6024 suffered no serious damage, passing a steam test just over a fortnight later and resuming main line passenger working on 4 May.

In the light of subsequent reductions in the loading gauge for steam locomotives to operate on the national network, the 6024 Preservation Society had no alternative but to lower the height of the chimney, safety valve cover and cab roof. Arguably, these modifications are not particularly obvious to the casual observer and, in the author's opinion, scarcely spoil the engine's appearance. No. 6023 is being

Opposite: A 'King' on the
Southern – unthinkable
in BR days! Flying the
Union flag for HM The
Queen's Golden Jubilee,
No. 6024 runs round its
train at Alresford on the
Mid-Hants Railway (the
Watercress Line), on
2 June 2002.
(Dick Franklin)

Left: Unusually, so it seems,
for a steam railtour, the
'Flying Dutchman' special
ran on a beautiful day,
9 November 1996. With
a heavyweight train of 13
carriages. No. 6024 is seen
early in the day on the down
relief line west of Slough.
(Geoff Rixon)

similarly treated, but one can understand
the reluctance of the NRM to carry out
such alterations to the GWR's flagship
locomotive, No. 6000 *King George V*, hence
the unlikelihood of this engine ever
returning to the main line.

Graham Ward, who works for DB
Schenker, formerly EWS, and is actively
involved with Didcot Railway Centre, has
fired on No. 6024 several times and hopes
to do the same on No. 6023 when this takes
to the main line in 2011. Graham describes
his experiences with 6024 as follows:

'Over the last ten years or so I have
been privileged to be involved with
the operation of No. 6024 *King Edward I*
many times on main line metals. I have
covered most of the routes worked by
the "King" class in the old steam days
and also some new routes now available

Left: Against the backdrop
of Didcot Power Station,
No. 6024 undertakes
wrong-line working as
it approaches Culham, a
route off-limits to 'Kings' in
GWR days and for most of
their BR days. It was on its
way from Paddington to
Oxford and Stratford upon
Avon on 24 April 1994,
during its initial five-year
spell on the main line.
(Dick Franklin)

Right: 'Kings' never reached Chester in BR days and, with the station looking as it does in this picture, there would have been no great incentive! However, No. 6024 ventured there on 27 March 1999, where it is seen at Platform 6. (Gwynne Parry)

Opposite: Fifty years earlier, No. 6018 King Henry VI would not have faced the eyesore of overhead electrification apparatus as it passed through Harringay in North London during the 1948 Locomotive Exchanges. However, we must be grateful that steam locomotives such as No. 6024, pictured hauling the 'Royal Sovereign' railtour in December 1998, are allowed under the wires today. (Geoff Rixon)

to "Kings" such as Bristol–Carmarthen, London–Birmingham via Oxford, and most notably, west from Plymouth into Cornwall.

Unfortunately, I have no experience of any other members of the class as No. 6000 was retired from service before I was accepted into the "steam link" of EWS drivers although following the epic restoration of No. 6023 *King Edward II* I may gain experience of the single-chimney, original version.

I am very proud to have worked with many ex-Tyseley enginemen over the last 30-odd years, many of whom worked on "Kings" regularly in their final years before withdrawal in 1962. Their advice and tips have been invaluable to me in my efforts to keep No. 6024 going well for new generations to enjoy.

On climbing aboard No. 6024 the first

thing that strikes you is the length of the firebox and also the size of the boiler. The "throw" from the shovel to the front of the grate is fully twelve feet. When people visit the cab at station stops they always gaze into the fire and ask: "How do you get the coal right down there?"

The boiler appears to look even bigger these days as the locomotive has to carry a specially lowered chimney, safety valve and cab roof. This is to comply with modern gauge clearances which restrict the height limit to 13ft 1in. As built, the "Kings" stood at 13ft 4 7/8in, and the same applies to No. 6023.

Firing a "King" is at first quite daunting. I had fired on preserved "Castles" Nos 5051 *Earl Bathurst* and 5029 *Nunney Castle* many times, but the effort needed to feed the front of No. 6024's firebox meant stepping up a gear.

It really is vital to have good quality coal to start with. You are on a hiding to nothing with poor coal and, yes, we have had some trips when the quality and size of the coal has been awful. It is quite simply a lottery with coal supplies these days. Two batches from supposedly the same source can burn altogether differently! All sorts have been tried by the 6024 Preservation Society, with imports from Russia and Columbia seeming the best. Home supply from Daw Mill in the Midlands will do the job but produces clouds of black smoke which of course is environmentally unfriendly these days.

If the coal is good then the other key to the job is keeping the shape of the fire right. "Kings", like most locomotives, need a large mound of coal in the "back end" i.e. inside the doors for about four

feet down the firebox and level with the firehole. The task then is to maintain a slope down under the brick arch to the front of the firebox. Problems start if you end up with a heap of coal under the arch which stops coal reaching the front. Holes can form then at the front, drawing in cold air from below and steam pressure will drop quickly. The middle of the fire can also burn away swiftly when the locomotive is working hard on a gradient. So you can see that firing No. 6024 at speed with a white-hot fire blinding you is no easy job.

On my first few trips I encountered all these problems but with experience you can learn to fire "to the pressure gauge". If pressure drops it is usually insufficient coal at the front and so six or eight shovelfuls must be aimed rapidly at the front corners. If the fire shape is right but pressure still drops, clinkers on the grate are forming and the pricker fireiron must be used to break them up to allow air through the grate. Another problem of operating on today's railways arises here. If you are running "under the wires" the fireirons cannot be used because of the danger of electrocution, should the fireiron touch the 250,000 volt cable.

Luckily, few trips with No. 6024 have included electrified routes. This illustrates how running steam on the main line today differs from the old "steam days". The environment on the railways is so different with no facilities available unless specially arranged.

I am told by the old colleagues of mine that some stations, e.g. Banbury, had a "King" pricker left at the trackside stopping point. This was because it was easier for the fireman to lift it off the ground and use it in the fire than to wrestle with it off the rack on top of the tender. Remember that it was, and still is, about 14ft long! We certainly don't have this convenience left for us today, although of course we do have the enthusiastic support crew lads who make life a lot easier for the main line crew these days.

So, on a good day with fine coal, firing No. 6024 can be one of the most rewarding challenges imaginable. To be

Left: The relative size of 'Kings' compared with 'Castles' is apparent in this view at Cockwood harbour, between Kingswear and Bristol, as No. 6024 King Edward I pilots No. 5051 Earl Bathurst on the first leg of the 'Great Britain' railtour from Penzance to Thurso on 7 March 2007. (Peter Zabek)

Above: Steam locomotives of different ancestry are used to haul the 'Torbay Express' specials between Bristol and Kingswear, but on 27 September 2009 there was very appropriate motive power in the shape of No. 6024. (Peter Zabek)

Right: Wearing the 'Bristolian' headboard, but departing from the original concept by travelling on the up relief line and hauling a larger number of carriages, No. 6024 presents an awesome sight as it leaves Sonning Cutting and heads for Twyford on 28 August 2010. (Peter Zabek)

on the locomotive with pressure "on the mark" while in full cry on Hatton Bank or on the Devon hills is awesome. But on a day with poor coal it can be a different story. You just want to reach the destination and get off the footplate!

I have also driven No. 6024 in recent years, mostly on the well-known "Torbay Express" specials between Bristol and Kingswear.

One characteristic of the locomotive which it has always possessed is immediately apparent. The regulator valve is very stiff to operate. The legendary enthusiast Kenneth Leech experienced this in 1959 and recorded this in his famous co-authored work entitled *Portraits of 'Kings'*. My old colleagues Dick Potts and Dennis Herbert also say that it was probably the worst "King" to drive. When starting away the pilot valve opens easily but it is impossible to open the main valve unless the "cut-off" is brought back to about 25 per cent. The main valve can be opened once the train is moving and the cut-off can then be adjusted to suit. The main valve is best left just open as No. 6024 is a strong engine and will handle most duties these days with the cut-off at around 20 per cent. The locomotive will take the "Torbay Express" over Whiteball on 35 per cent cut-off with the main valve just open and sounding superb. A similar setting is used on the return "Torbay Express" with the climb up Torre Bank being the start of the run and the echoes are roused as No. 6024 storms past the Victorian terraces and guest houses of Torquay.

I just hope that No. 6023 will give the same pleasure that No. 6024 has given over the years. With a single chimney the coal and firing issues I have mentioned will be even more important. Dick Potts has warned me that it will be very hard work – time will tell, hopefully very soon!'

No. 6023 *King Edward II*

This locomotive entered service in June 1930, initially being allocated to Newton Abbot depot and, apart from being re-allocated to Plymouth (Laira) for a month in late 1936, remained at Newton Abbot until February 1949.

No. 6023 was then transferred again to Laira, this time spending more than seven years there, before moving on to Old Oak Common in August 1956. In September 1960, the engine was sent to its final shed in BR service, Cardiff (Canton), from where it was withdrawn in June 1962, having covered 1,554,201 miles.

It should be pointed out that transfers of 'Kings' between depots often occurred as a result of visits to Swindon Works for overhaul. These overhauls normally involved boiler changes, a float of new or refurbished 'King' boilers being maintained at Swindon to speed up the time when the locomotive was out of service. No. 6023 had 13 different boilers during its working life, its current boiler being fitted in June 1960 having been built in 1954 and originally carried by No. 6012 and later by No. 6003.

After initial storage out of service at Canton shed, No. 6023 was dispatched to Swindon and had reached the reception area there by mid-August 1962. As mentioned earlier, it was initially purchased by T.W. Ward of Briton Ferry in West Wales on 10 October 1962. It was then realised that the engine was too heavy to make this final journey and the sale was cancelled, with the locomotive being sold instead to Woodham Bros at Barry Docks on 26 November 1962.

Once at Barry, No. 6023, along with No. 6024 and some 200 other locomotives, languished in the sea air, gradually rusting away. However, when the process of rescuing locomotives from Barry scrapyard for future preservation became well established, attention turned to the two 'Kings'. No. 6023 had the newer boiler in terms of usage, having run just over 300,000 miles since its construction in 1954, whereas No. 6024's boiler had over 400,000 miles on the clock (much the same as No. 6000's).

Unfortunately, No. 6023's rear driving wheels became derailed during a shunting operation within the scrapyard

Right: Two former drivers of No. 6023 King Edward II in GWR days were C.O. Davis and D.J. Mann. Both men had the honour of driving Royal trains and ended their careers at Newton Abbot depot, working expresses to Paddington and to Shrewsbury. On the left is Driver Davis who began his railway career as a cleaner in 1897. He became a fireman the following year and was promoted to driver in 1912, retiring in 1945. Driver Mann, on the right, also began his railway career as a cleaner in 1897. He was promoted to fireman in 1899 and to driver in 1912, retiring around the same time as Driver Davis. (The Railway Magazine)

locomotives were constantly being moved around in order to release ones sold to preservationists), and the problem was overcome by slicing through the bottom parts of this pair of wheels with a cutter's torch. This was regarded at the time as rendering the locomotive unsalvageable, with the result that No. 6024 was chosen for preservation in preference to No. 6023. Parts from the latter were subsequently purchased for use on other ex-GWR locomotives. Luckily, the frames of No. 6023 had not become distorted as a result

of the locomotive only resting on two sets of driving wheels instead of all three.

Fortune finally shone on No. 6023 in 1982 when the Barry Steam Locomotive Action Group purchased the locomotive for £15,000, this appeal having been led by Mike Cokayne, who had to fight off a great deal of criticism from railway enthusiasts at the time, for pursuing what they said was a hopeless project. The intention was for it to be taken to Brighton for restoration. By this time, the locomotive's condition was dire because, apart from

the destruction of the rear driving wheel set and the loss of so many parts, it had remained at Barry for almost ten years longer than No. 6024.

However, before the engine was moved from Barry, the Brighton project was aborted and No. 6023 was sold to Harveys, the sherry manufacturer, for £21,000 who presented it to the Brunel Engineering Centre Trust (BECT) for restoration under a Government Manpower Services Scheme. The locomotive was taken to the former Fish Dock siding at Bristol Temple Meads station.

Above: Newly allocated to Cardiff (Canton) shed, No. 6023 King Edward II approaches Twyford with the up 'Capitals United Express' from Swansea to Paddington on 10 September 1960. (Ken Wightman)

Above: Stripped, rusting and with a rear driving wheel cut through (the less wrecked one of the pair, believe it or not!) this picture shows the desperate state of No. 6023 during its latter days at Barry scrapyard.
(Peter Zabek)

Restoration work commenced there in 1985 but came to an abrupt halt in August 1988 following the cancellation of the Manpower Services Scheme, following which the BECT was given notice to quit the Fish Dock siding. Funding ceased and some parts, which were being worked on by outside contractors were apparently scrapped, notably the splashers, cab sides and tender tank.

In 1989, the Great Western Society learned that No. 6023 was up for sale and bought the surviving components for around £16,000, the price including the cost of transportation by rail in wagons from Bristol to Didcot. What amounted to little more than a kit of parts reached Didcot

shed in March 1990. With the luxury of ample covered accommodation, the lengthy process of restoration to working order could begin in earnest, subject to the usual financial constraints.

The first priority was to create a running chassis and by February 1992 a complete set of new springs had been delivered. A new running plate, splashers, cab sides and cab roof had also arrived.

In addition, orders started to be placed for the manufacture of new motion gear, where the original parts were missing, and for the refurbishment of surviving components. The most costly order was for a new set of rear driving wheels

and these arrived in February 1994, although not fitted until July 1995. In all, thousands of new fittings, many of them small items, have had to be obtained and the task of restoration would have been even more difficult had it not been for the existence of the other two surviving 'Kings' and the valuable co-operation of their custodians.

The Great Western Society decided that No. 6023 should revert to the single blastpipe and single chimney arrangement, which it possessed in the early 1950s, the necessary alterations being completed in 1997. This arrangement had brought about significant performance improvements, albeit not matching those subsequently achieved by the installation of a double blastpipe and double chimney, through the fitting of a longer but narrower chimney liner and a smaller diameter blast pipe. When the engine left Barry, it had no chimney, this having been removed at the scrapyard to replace the missing one on No. 6024 which had been removed to replace that on No. 6000!

Obtaining a single chimney proved extremely difficult until one was found in the garden of a former First World War pilot in Northamptonshire where it was being used as a plant pot! This is now carried by No. 6023. To maintain late 1940s/early 1950s authenticity, a step iron has been welded to the smokebox door and the mechanical lubricator has reverted to the original position behind the outside steam pipe. To further distinguish No. 6023 from the other two surviving 'Kings', the locomotive will initially run in BR blue livery, a feature which would not be authentic on Nos 6000 and 6024, both of which are technically restricted to wearing BR green livery due to having the double blastpipe and double chimney arrangement.

Below: With brand-new cab, splashers and fire iron tunnel. No. 6023 starts to take shape at Didcot depot, while No. 6024 keeps it company. Harveys' involvement in rescuing No. 6023 is recorded in the hoarding seen at the rear of the engine shed. No. 6024 is displaying, on its front valance, the GWR shed code for Old Oak Common (PDN, the abbreviation for Paddington). (Great Western Society)

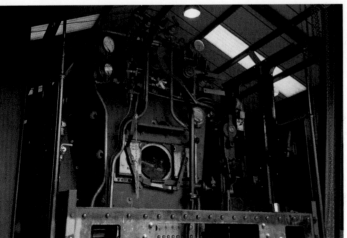

Far left: No. 6023's new cab controls and associated pipework were trialled in situ before the boiler was removed for retubing, etc., in order to obtain the maximum amount of time from its boiler 'ticket'. (Great Western Society)

Left: This is the new steam fountain casting, which stands on top of the firebox inside the cab. The original casting disappeared while the locomotive was in Barry scrapyard. (Frank Dumbleton/ Great Western Society)

Right: Certain electronic equipment is necessary in steam locomotives passed for main line running today, and this photograph shows the AWS/TPWS system being installed beneath the driver's seat in the cab of No. 6023. (Great Western Society)

Far right: This view, taken inside the smokebox shows the four-row superheater elements, above which is the header, with the regulator box on top. (Frank Dumbleton/ Great Western Society)

Right: The new ashpan is lowered on to the frames for trial fitting on 12 June 2010. It was not possible to attach this to the firebox beforehand because the crane in the Lifting Shop did not have sufficient height to raise the boiler with the ashpan attached. (Frank Dumbleton/ Great Western Society)

The original boiler mountings were built to satisfy the original 13ft 4 7/8in loading gauge, but this has now been reduced to 13ft 1in on the national rail network. Consequently, No. 6023 has two sets of fittings: original-height chimney, safety valve bonnet and cab roof for operation on heritage lines and an alternative set reduced in height by just under four inches, for main line running. The locomotive has also been fitted with the obligatory TPWS (Train Protection Warning System) and OTMR (On Train Monitoring Recorder – comparable to an aircraft's 'black box') required for currently operating on the national network. However, unless circumstances change in the future, No. 6023 will not be air-braked, unlike No. 6024.

To maintain its seven-year main line boiler 'ticket' for as long as possible, restoration of the boiler and firebox (retubing, replacement stays, etc.) was left until last. This may have confused visitors to Didcot Railway Centre in Summer 2003 when the locomotive, minus its tender, was displayed outside the works in apparently complete condition, looking as though it was almost ready to be fired up. Three years later, No. 6023, this time re-united with its tender, appeared even more complete when displayed outside in July 2006.

Yet a few weeks later a start had been made on dismantling it and the boiler was lifted from the frames in

he following December! It then joined he queue of boilers at Didcot awaiting ttention while work continued on the emainder of the locomotive.

Repairs to the boiler started in earnest in 2009 but the extremely cold weather in the early part of 2010 slowed down the process. Nevertheless, on 15 March the boiler passed its hydraulic est and on the 28 March the first fire or 48 years was lit in the firebox.

A further significant milestone was reached on 12 April 2010 when a steam test was carried out on the boiler which was passed to 260lb psi. After a short delay caused by the fitting of a new ash pan the boiler was lifted back on to the frames on 24 July 2010 and No. 6023 became a complete locomotive again.

By Spring 2011, the engine had become fully operational at last and was officially unveiled at Didcot on April 2 by Steve Davies of the NRM, in front of 3,000 enthusiasts. A few days later it was wonderful to see Nos 6023 and 6024 reunited once more, given that they have spent much of their lives together. They were built alongside one another in 1930, allocated to the same depots (Newton Abbot, Laira, Old Oak Common and Canton) for most of the time between 1934 and 1962, stood together at Swindon Works following withdrawal, and ended up in the same scrapyard/ sanctuary – a remarkable, long-standing association.

It has cost around £750,000 and taken over 400,000 man hours to return this 'no-hoper' to operation, which will provide the opportunity to see a single-chimney 'King' in action for the first time in over 50 years. No. 6023 had a period of running-in at Didcot after which it moved to the Mid-Norfolk Railway to accumulate further mileage in June and July. The locomotive has been subjected to various tests by the Vehicle Acceptance Body (VAB) which included checking the TPWS and OTMR equipment, and the carrying out of a loaded test run before a main line certificate was issued.

No. 6023 will normally be based at Didcot, which will not be out of

Above: On 28 March 2010, Richard Croucher (Great Western Society Chairman) and Dennis Howells (Project Manager), put No. 6023 in steam for the first time in 48 years. (Frank Dumbleton/ Great Western Society)

Left: Lowered on to the frames by Didcot's 50-tonne Lifting Shop crane, which is only two years younger than the locomotive, the boiler of No. 6023 is reunited with the new ashpan on 24 July 2010. (Frank Dumbleton/ Great Western Society)

Right: No. 6023 stands on Didcot's turntable ready for the commisioning ceremony to begin. (Frank Dumbleton/ Great Western Society)

keeping because, although no 'Kings' were ever allocated there, No. 6023 and other members of the class certainly visited the depot, not only when they were used on the Didcot–Paddington semi-fasts, but also on running-in turns from Swindon.

There is a certain irony in the Great Western Society having purchased and restored No. 6023 for, in the July 1967 issue of *The Railway Magazine*, the society was reported to have formed a 'King Preservation Fund' to rescue No. 6023. The chairman at that time subsequently issued a denial, which included the immortal words: 'The Society would only consider purchasing a 'King' in the event of official notification being received from the proper authorities that 6000 was not being saved.' Hindsight is a wonderful thing because, had the appeal supposedly launched by the society not been bogus, it could have saved itself a considerable amount of money and effort!

Right: Flanked by No. 4965 Rood Ashton Hall and No. 5043 Earl of Mount Edgcumbe (but Tyseley-based) and Didcot-based No. 5051 Earl Bathurst No. 6023 awaits formal commisioning into service. (Frank Dumbleton/ Great Western Society)

Above: No. 6023 King Edward II passes its old wrecked wheelset at Didcot Railway Centre on 2 April 2011. (Frank Dumbleton/Great Western Society)

Right: On the sunnier day of the launch weekend, No. 6023 King Edward II works a passenger train on Didcot's main demonstration line on 3 April 2011. (Frank Dumbleton/Great Western Society)

Overleaf: Nos. 6023 and 6024 double-head at Didcot on 23 April 2011 during a maintenance visit by No. 6024, whose cut-down boiler mountings are clearly evident. (Peter Zabek)

Postscript

There is a school of thought that the 'Kings' were produced purely for publicity purposes in order that the GWR could regain the mantle of having the most powerful express passenger locomotives. However, this view can easily be challenged. The GWR did not need to produce as many as 30 of these locomotives to achieve that objective. The company could have made do with far fewer, perhaps even just one (as in the case of *The Great Bear*). Thirty was a relatively large number, comparing well with 38 'Princess Coronations' ('Duchesses') and 35 A4s, both classes being required for a much larger network. Indeed, there were only 16 'Lord Nelsons' and 13 'Princess Royals' built.

Another point of criticism in some quarters is the fact that the building of a relatively small number of 'Kings' (30) over a short time span (1927–1930), compared with the large number of 'Castles' (171), with new ones being constructed over such a long time period (1923–1950), is indicative of the 'Kings' being an unsuccessful class compared with the 'Castles'. This view fails to take into account the fact that, in the light of results obtained from the Swindon stationary test plant, it was more efficient to put 'Castles' on well-loaded, rather than lightly loaded trains.

Utilising 'Castles' so that they operated at their optimum capacity was therefore the objective, with the result that few trains were in fact beyond the capabilities of a 'Castle'. Nevertheless, there were undoubtedly a sufficient number of heavily loaded trains, such as the 'Cornish Riviera Express' and some London–Birmingham two-hour expresses, to warrant the construction of a limited number of more powerful locomotives, which could also operate at their optimum capacity, i.e. having the ability to haul these heavily loaded trains, economically. Thirty was deemed to be the right quantity of 'Kings' needed.

Right: There is much activity at Didcot shed on 29 April 2011 with newly restored steam railmotor No. 93 keeping company with both working kings, Nos 6023 and 6024.
(Frank Dumbleton)

A further indication of the success of the 'Kings' is the fact that they were generally revered by employees, and not just by the footplate crews. Indeed, it is said that at Swindon Works, there was considerable reluctance on the part of the breakers to cut up these fine engines. Collett's 'Kings' were undoubtedly one of the most important classes of British steam locomotives, sharing the honours with such iconic express locomotive types as the Bulleid Pacifics, Stanier 'Coronations' and Gresley A4s of the other railway companies/BR regions.

Finally, the Royal Mail issued a set of stamps in the summer of 2010 illustrating six locomotives representing 'Great British Railways'. Incredibly, perhaps, neither a Bulleid Pacific nor a Gresley A4 was featured, a 'King Arthur' and Gresley A1 (forerunner of the A3) being chosen instead to represent the SR and LNER.

However, there was no surprise over the GWR example selected – a 'King' of course! The Royal Mail commentary on the stamp stated: 'The 'Kings' were the GWR's star locomotives, equally at home on heavy holiday trains and crack business expresses. Publicised as the UK's most powerful express engine, *King George V*, with its sleek lines, wowed crowds when touring the USA in 1927.' Full marks to the Royal Mail – an excellent summation!

Above: No. 6024 King Edward I makes a fine sight as it passes Little Bedwyn Lock on the Kennet & Avon Canal in Wiltshire, with the 'Flying Dutchman' railtour on 9 November 1996. (Peter Zabek)

Appendix

Numbers, names, build and withdrawal dates and disposals

No.	Name	Date built	Withdrawn	Disposal	Notes
6000	King George V	6/27	12/62	Preserved	1
6001	King Edward VII	7/27	9/62	Cox & Danks	
6002	King William IV	7/27	9/62	Cox & Danks	
6003	King George IV	7/27	6/62	Swindon Works	
6004	King George III	7/27	6/62	Swindon Works	
6005	King George II	7/27	11/62	Cashmores	
6006	King George I	2/28	2/62	Swindon Works	
6007	King William III	3/28	9/62	Cox & Danks	2
6008	King James II	3/28	6/62	Swindon Works	
6009	King Charles II	3/28	9/62	Cashmores	
6010	King Charles I	4/28	6/62	Swindon Works	
6011	King James I	4/28	12/62	Swindon Works	
6012	King Edward VI	4/28	9/62	Cox & Danks	
6013	King Henry VIII	5/28	6/62	Swindon Works	
6014	King Henry VII	5/28	9/62	Cox & Danks	3
6015	King Richard III	6/28	9/62	Cox & Danks	
6016	King Edward V	6/28	9/62	Cashmores	
6017	King Edward IV	6/28	7/62	Cox & Danks	
6018	King Henry VI	6/28	12/62	Swindon Works	4
6019	King Henry V	7/28	9/62	Cashmores	
6020	King Henry IV	5/30	7/62	Cox & Danks	
6021	King Richard II	6/30	9/62	Cashmores	
6022	King Edward III	6/30	9/62	Cox & Danks	
6023	King Edward II	6/30	6/62	Woodham Bros	5
6024	King Edward I	6/30	6/62	Woodham Bros	6
6025	King Henry III	7/30	12/62	Swindon Works	
6026	King John	7/30	9/62	Swindon Works	
6027	King Richard I	7/30	9/62	Cox & Danks	
6028	King George VI	7/30	11/62	Birds	7
6029	King Edward VIII	8/30	7/62	Cashmores	8

Notes:

1 Part of the National Collection – in main line service 1971–1987.
2 Rebuilt in 1936 following serious damage in the Shrivenham accident.
3 Semi-streamlined in 1935, with most streamlining parts later removed.
4 Temporarily returned to service 22–28 April 1963.
5 Purchased from scrap merchant for preservation and returned to service in 2011.
6 Purchased from scrap merchant for preservation and returned to service in 1990.
7 Name changed from *King Henry II* in January 1937.
8 Name changed from *King Stephen* in May 1936.

Shed allocations

No.	First shed	1939	1949	1957	1960	Final shed
6000	Old Oak	Exeter	Bath Rd	Old Oak	Old Oak	Old Oak
6001	Old Oak	Old Oak	Old Oak	Staff Rd	Staff Rd	Staff Rd
6002	Laira	Exeter	Laira	Old Oak	Laira	Staff Rd
6003	Old Oak	Old Oak	Old Oak	Old Oak	Old Oak	Canton
6004	Laira	Laira	Staff Rd	Laira	Old Oak	Old Oak
6005	Old Oak	Staff Rd	Staff Rd	Staff Rd	Staff Rd	Old Oak
6006	Laira	Staff Rd	Staff Rd	Staff Rd	Staff Rd	Staff Rd
6007	Old Oak	Laira	Laira	Laira	Staff Rd	Staff Rd
6008	Laira	Staff Rd	Staff Rd	Laira	Staff Rd	Staff Rd
6009	Old Oak	Old Oak	Old Oak	Old Oak	Old Oak	Old Oak
6010	Laira	Laira	Laira	Laira	Old Oak	Canton
6011	Old Oak	Bath Rd	Staff Rd	Staff Rd	Staff Rd	Old Oak
6012	Newton A	Laira	Laira	Old Oak	Old Oak	Staff Rd
6013	Old Oak	Old Oak	Old Oak	Old Oak	Laira	Staff Rd
6014	Newton A	Old Oak	Old Oak	Staff Rd	Staff Rd	Staff Rd
6015	Old Oak	Old Oak	Old Oak	Old Oak	Old Oak	Staff Rd
6016	Laira	Laira	Laira	Old Oak	Laira	Staff Rd
6017	Old Oak	Bath Rd	Old Oak	Laira	Staff Rd	Staff Rd
6018	Laira	Newton A	Bath Rd	Old Oak	Old Oak	Old Oak
6019	Staff Rd	Laira	Bath Rd	Old Oak	Canton	Staff Rd
6020	Laira	Laira	Laira	Staff Rd	Staff Rd	Staff Rd
6021	Old Oak	Old Oak	Old Oak	Laira	Old Oak	Old Oak
6022	Laira	Laira	Laira	Old Oak	Staff Rd	Staff Rd
6023	Newton A	Newton A	Newton A	Old Oak	Old Oak	Canton
6024	Laira	Newton A	Laira	Old Oak	Old Oak	Canton
6025	Old Oak	Old Oak	Laira	Laira	Old Oak	Old Oak
6026	Old Oak	Bath Rd	Laira	Laira	Laira	Old Oak
6027	Old Oak	Old Oak	Laira	Laira	Staff Rd	Staff Rd
6028	Old Oak	Old Oak	Old Oak	Old Oak	Canton	Old Oak
6029	Old Oak	Laira	Laira	Laira	Old Oak	Old Oak

Abbreviations:
Old Oak = Old Oak Common (Paddington)
Bath Rd = Bath Road, Bristol
Newton A = Newton Abbot, Devon
Laira = Plymouth
Canton = Cardiff
Staff Rd = Stafford Road, Wolverhampton

Acknowledgements and Bibliography

This book would not have seen the light of day had it not been for the help of many old and new friends as well as some commercial and charitable organisations. With apologies to anyone I have missed out, I would like to thank the following:

John Scott-Morgan, Neil Davenport, Bob Bridger, Dennis Howells, Graham Ward, Dick Potts, Michael Mensing, Michael Bentley, Alan Sainty, Peter Zabek, Mike Pope, Brian Hicks, Frank Dumbleton, John Beckett, Roy Hobbs, Geoff Rixon, Jim Oatway, John Cramp, Bruce Jenkins, Michael Allen, Ian Nash, Dick Franklin, Alan Jarvis, Nick Lera, Jim Jarvis, Les Folkard, David Lemar, Paddy Baker, Bill Piggott, Phil Cox, Fred Jeanes, Adrian Vaughan, David Clark, Roy Vandersteen, Gwynne Parry, Barry Hoper (Transport Treasury), Laurence Waters (Great Western Trust, Didcot), Martin Jenkins (Online Transport Archive), Roger Jones (Light Rail Transit Association (LRTA)), The Cinema & Television Benevolent Fund, Shrivenham Heritage Centre, Newbury Racecourse Co, and the Bytown Railway Society of Canada.

The following publications have provided invaluable information for this book and are recommended for further reading:

W.G. Chapman, *The 'King' of Railway Locomotives* (GWR, 1928)

O.S. Nock, *The GWR Stars, Castles & Kings* (David & Charles, 1980)

Rex Coffin, *Kings of the Great Western 1927–1977* (6000 Locomotive Association, 1977)

O.S. Nock, *Engine 6000* (David & Charles, 1972)

Peter Semmens, *History of the Great Western Railway* (Guild Publishing, 1985)

Bryan Holden & Kenneth H. Leech, *Portraits of 'Kings'* (Moorland Publishing, 1979)

O.S. Nock, *Speed Records on Britain's Railways* (David & Charles, 1971)

O.S. Nock, *British Railways in Action* (Thomas Nelson & Sons, 1956)

O.S. Nock, *The Limited* (George Allen & Unwin, 1979)

G.C. Wood, *6000 King George V – A Chronology* (6000 Locomotive Association, 1972)

W.G. Chapman, *Loco's of 'The Royal Road'* (GWR, 1936)

C.G. Brown, *6024 King Edward I* (Ian Allan, 1991)

Henry Coates, *A Western Monarch* (6024 Preservation Society, 2007)

Brian Dodd, *Great Preserved Locomotives (7) 'King' Class No. 6000* (Ian Allan, 1987)

Bill Peto, *Peto's Register of GWR Locomotives, Vol. 1, King 4-6-0s* (Irwell Press, 1995)

A. Kingdom, *The Newton Abbot Blitz* (Oxford Publishing Co, 1979)

Various magazines including *The Railway Magazine*, *Trains Illustrated*, *Meccano Magazine*, *Railway Wonders of the World*, and the *Great Western Echo* (the magazine of the Great Western Society).

Right: No. 6023 King Edward II stands alongside Didcot shed in exactly the same position, and wearing the same blue livery, as it had done 61 years earlier when visiting Didcot on a running-in turn following overhaul at Swindon Works.
(Peter Zabek)

Index